PERILS OF PROGRESS
Environmental Disasters in the Twentieth Century

Andrew L. Jenks
California State University, Long Beach

Prentice Hall

Boston   Columbus   Indianapolis   New York   San Francisco   Upper Saddle River
Amsterdam   Cape Town   Dubai   London   Madrid   Milan   Munich   Paris
Montreal   Toronto   Delhi   Mexico City   Sao Paulo   Sydney
Hong Kong   Seoul   Singapore   Taipei   Tokyo

Editorial Director: Craig Campanella
Editorial Assistant: Amanda Dykstra
Executive Editor: Jeff Lasser
Director of Marketing: Brandy Dawson
Senior Marketing Manager: Maureen Prado-Roberts
Production Manager: Meghan DeMaio
Creative Director: Jayne Conte
Cover Designer: Suzanne Behnke
Manager, Visual Research: Beth Brenzel
Manager, Rights and Permissions: Zina Arabia
Image Permission Coordinator: Rita Wenning
Manager, Cover Visual Research & Permissions: Karen Sanatar
Cover Art: Igor Kostin/Sygma/Corbis
Maps: Alliance Publishing
Full-Service Project Management: Sadagoban Balaji
Composition: Integra Software Services
Printer/Binder/Cover Printer: Courier Companies

This book was set in Palatino.

Chernobyl – The Aftermath
Liquidators cleared radioactive debris off the roof of number 4 reactor, throwing it on the ground where it would later be covered by the sarcophagus. These "biological robots," who ran on the top of the roof of the damaged site, in Chernobyl, could stay no longer than 60 seconds (announced by a wailing siren.) As a general rule, they only had time to place themselves by a pile of debris, lift a shovel-load and throw it on among the ruins of the reactor. Normally, the liquidators ascended the roof only once because the radiation dose they received was the maximum authorized dosage a human being should receive in a lifetime

Credits and acknowledgments borrowed from other sources and reproduced, with permission, in this textbook appear on appropriate page within text.

Library of Congress Cataloging-in-Publication Data
Jenks, Andrew L.
  Perils of progress : environmental disasters in the twentieth century/Andrew L. Jenks.—1st ed.
     p. cm.
Includes bibliographical references and index.
ISBN-13: 978-0-13-603802-3 (alk. paper)
ISBN-10: 0-13-603802-6 (alk. paper)
   1. Disasters.   2. Environmental disasters. I. Title.
HC79.D45J46 2010
363.73809'04—dc22

                                                    2010003397

10 9 8 7 6 5 4 3 2 1

Prentice Hall
is an imprint of

www.pearsonhighered.com

ISBN 13: 978-0-13-603802-3
ISBN 10:   0-13-603802-6

Contents

Foreword

Connections: Key Themes in World History focuses on specific issues of world historical significance from antiquity to the present by employing a combination of explanatory narrative, primary sources, questions relating to those sources, a summary analysis ("Making Connections"), and further points to ponder, all of which combine to enable readers to discover some of the most important driving forces in world history. The increasingly rapid pace and specialization of historical inquiry has created an ever-widening gap between professional publications and general surveys, especially surveys of world history. The purpose of *Connections* is to bridge that gap by placing the latest research and debates on selected topics of global historical significance, as well as some of the evidence upon which historians base their insights, into a form and context that is comprehensible to students and general readers alike.

Two pedagogical principles infuse this series. First, students master world history most easily if allowed to focus on specific themes and issues. Such themes, by their very specificity, as well as because of their general application, enable students to perceive and understand the overall patterns and meaning of our shared global past more clearly than is possible through reading, by itself, a massive world history textbook. Second, students learn best when asked to think critically about what they are studying. So far as the study of history is concerned, critical thinking necessarily involves analysis of primary sources.

To that end, we offer a series of brief, tightly focused books that embrace a radical simplicity and a provocative format. Each book goes to the heart of a key theme, phenomenon, or issue in world history—something that has connected humans across cultures, continents, and time spans. By actively engaging with this material, the reader comes to understand in a nuanced and meaningful manner how often distantly located human cultures have been connected to one another as key actors in the epic story of world history.

Alfred J. Andrea
Series Editor
Professor Emeritus of History
The University of Vermont

Series Editor's Preface

"Vermont: We were green before green became cool." That aphorism graced a number of T-shirts and hats in downtown Burlington on Saturday, June 13, 2009, as thousands of Vermonters and visitors alike enjoyed the sunny weather and the last several days of another successful jazz festival. And who would be so foolish as to deny the people of this state that boast? This is the land of Ben and Jerry's ice cream, made from family farm–produced hormone-free milk. This is the land of farmers' markets in almost every village and town, where one can purchase seasonally correct, organic, free-range, antibiotic-free meats, cheeses, eggs, vegetables, and fruits. This is the state that in 1970, under the active leadership of an otherwise conservative Republican governor, passed the pioneering Land Use and Development Act, better known as Act 250, that established nine district environment commissions tasked with reviewing closely and judging the merits of all permit applications for any development project of 10 acres or more, to ensure that such projects would not have an adverse effect on the environment, especially in regard to water and air pollution. This is the state that sent to Washington Republican senator Robert Stafford, who, more than any other member of the Congress, was responsible for championing and protecting the integrity of national clean air and clean water legislation. Yes, this land of Birkenstock-wearing, Prius-driving, tofu-eating, tree-hugging environmentalists takes pride in its self-image: a state in which careful stewardship of the land trumps mindless pursuit of profits.

This stereotype might please Vermont chambers of commerce, and it certainly sells large amounts of pure maple syrup and other products whose "Made in Vermont" stamps carry a cachet that assures high prices and a ready clientele in urban upscale markets across the United States. But as any student of history instinctively knows, it cannot be and is not the whole story. To be sure, Vermont has known no environmental disasters of anywhere near the magnitude of the four highlighted in this marvelous little book. Nevertheless, this state, so well known for its environmental activism, faces toxic challenges that threaten the health and well-being of its residents.

The poisoning of some fish species in Lake Champlain, North America's sixth largest body of fresh water, by the effluent formerly discharged into the lake by International Paper's Ticonderoga Paper Mill in neighboring New York pales into insignificance when compared to the poisoning of Japan's Minamata Bay, described in Chapter 1. And yet Lake Champlain provides the drinking water for most of the people living along its shores, including the city of Burlington, and the toxic wastes discharged by the Ticonderoga Paper Mill remain on its fragile lakebed. What is more, chemicals sprayed on the lawns of Burlington and the towns and cities of Vermont, New York, and Quebec that border this immense body of water run into the lake and help feed a rapidly growing blue-green algae (Cyanobacteria) that is choking the lake and posing a serious threat to the health of humans and animals alike. To be sure, chemical fertilizers are only one source of the problem; even greater sources are the manure spread on frozen fields near the lake and the phosphorus-rich gray water of washing machines. Currently, the state is commemorating the 400th anniversary of Samuel de Champlain's "discovery" of the lake. Thanks to the "progress" of development, much of the shoreline has changed substantially since 1609. One wonders if, despite the best efforts of the Lake Champlain Land Trust to buy up portions of the shoreline to serve as buffer areas against this chemical invasion and the equally active efforts of the state's Agency of Natural Resources to regulate and educate, the lake will be choked into a state of near or total necrosis by 2109.

Vermont has nothing to compare with Love Canal, which, as described in painful detail in Chapter 2, is a prime example of the human cost of irresponsible toxic waste "management." But Burlington has its Pine Street Barge Canal, which in 1983 became a local Superfund poster child. In the mid-1800s, as Burlington's lakeside lumber business boomed, a local entrepreneur transformed a "miasmic frog pond," what today we would call a vital wetland, into a barge canal, complete with a drawbridge, that linked the vessels plying the lake with nearby lumber mills and the railway system that ran along the lake. When the lumber industry went bust in the 1890s, a number of other businesses, especially coal dealers, filled the void and occupied the area around the barge canal on Burlington's waterfront. A plant that converted coal and oil into gas for streetlights and home heating soon opened on the site, and it began the process of dumping coal tar and other equally dangerous waste products into the waters and on the surrounding wetlands of the canal until the plant ceased operations in 1966. The result was contamination by a lethal combination of heavy metals and chemicals. Given the slow process of scientific and bureaucratic investigation and review and the number of competing theories and voices, it took 20 years to find and execute an agreeable solution as to how to return the area to a reasonable state of nontoxicity. By 2004, eight acres of the most heavily contaminated sediments were capped and serious efforts at habitat restoration were completed. Some coal tar gases continue to be released in one area, but by and large the means taken seem worth the wait and expended resources. Monitoring of the site continues.

Without any major chemical plants, Vermont has little reason to fear a Bhopal-like cloud of choking gasses descending on a sleeping community, as described in Chapter 3. But living as I do close to the railway tracks that run along the east coast of Lake Champlain, it is disquieting to see on a daily basis tanker cars containing a variety of deadly chemicals rolling along the tracks at any time of day or night, headed for unknown destinations. Our local fire department and other emergency responders are well trained for any eventuality, but one does have to wonder what would happen should there be an accident or act of terrorism. But in this world where "better things for better living . . . through chemistry," as the old DuPont advertising slogan boasted, is a reality, one has to trust the safeguards and probabilities. Toxic chemicals, whether we like it or not, are an integral part of our society and its economic infrastructure, and even supposedly isolated

The Pine Street Barge Canal with tanker cars full of chemicals in the background. (Alfred J. Andrea)

Shangri Las, such as Vermont, must bear the risk of living in close proximity to them.

That said, the cost of even relative safety is eternal vigilance. Yesterday's *Burlington Free Press* led with the story of a trash-to-energy debate concerning the plans of an electric utility and a major trash hauler to construct several plants where solid waste would be converted to energy. One does wonder what the effects on air quality will be, apart from undermining recycling and waste-reduction programs, especially if the known carcinogen dioxin is released. Needless to say, environmentalists and scientists are lining up on both sides of the debate. In this most imperfect of worlds, it is never easy to choose the best or least objectionable and least dangerous alternative. The Union Carbide pesticide plant in Bhopal, India, promised to produce cheap pesticides, which would be an integral component of the Green Revolution that would feed India's then hundreds of millions of people. Who could have foreseen the deadly fog that would descend on the city in December 1984?

Other than the near meltdown at Three Mile Island in 1979, the United States has been spared any nuclear power plant disaster, and certainly the Three Mile Island incident paled when compared with what took place at Chernobyl in April 1986, as we learn in Chapter 4. Surely both incidents seem so far away from Vermont, where so many folks heat at least partially with wood (thus adding to air pollution and resultant respiratory ailments in a substantial manner). But even bucolic Vermont has a nuclear power plant, Vermont Yankee. While its safety record is good, it is not spotless. More troubling is an Associated Press bulletin, which appeared in newspapers throughout the state, that the company that owns it and almost half of the nation's other nuclear reactors has not been setting aside sufficient funds for their inevitable and fast-approaching decommissioning and dismantlement, thus raising fears of safety and security risks.

As Andrew Jenks points out so well in this book, which studies four of this century's most infamous and deadly toxic disasters, progress comes at a great potential price, and that price can be multiplied many times over when pursuit of profits trumps prudence. Moreover, the tragedy can and will be exacerbated when civic and corporate leaders fail to acknowledge or adequately deal with the causes and consequences of a disaster.

It would be foolish for anyone in the twenty-first century to advocate a return to an earlier and putatively cleaner way of life. Humans have been poisoning their environment and themselves since at least the discovery of fire, and many of the agreeable benefits of contemporary life would not be available to so many so inexpensively were it not for the chemicals used in the production of those benefits and the energy from nuclear reactors that drives their machines. What is more, no place on earth, even such mythically pristine sites as Vermont, is totally free from the dangers of a toxic cataclysm. That noted, there is much that we, as responsible citizens, can and should do to reduce the inherent dangers of contemporary manufacture, and there is much that we can do to mitigate suffering if and when the next toxic disaster occurs.

This book should be read and carefully studied by anyone who is at all interested in furthering a clean and safe environment while simultaneously encouraging responsible manufacturing. Life as we know it demands both. But when reading this book, do not look for facile answers. They do not exist. What can be gained from this book, as is true of any nuanced study of the past conducted by a master historian, is insight and wisdom—two qualities that prepare us to anticipate and head off potential environmental disasters and, even, sad to say, meet and deal rationally with the next toxic apocalypse.

Alfred J. Andrea
Series Editor

About the Author

Dr. Andrew Jenks, an associate professor of history at California State University, Long Beach, is a specialist in Russian history, history of technology, and environmental history. In addition to publishing numerous articles in scholarly publications on a range of topics, he has authored a book on Russian national identity, *Russia in a Box: Art and Identity in an Age of Revolution*, Northern Illinois University Press, and is currently finishing a biography of the world's first man in space, Yuri Gagarin, *The Cosmonaut Who Couldn't Stop Smiling: Yuri Gagarin and the Many Faces of Modern Russia*, Northern Illinois University Press. Before receiving his Ph.D. in Russian history and history of technology from Stanford University in 2002, Jenks worked in the 1990s as a journalist and editor in Washington, D.C., where he covered NASA, EPA, secret military high-tech programs, and the emerging Internet business. He studied Russian language at the Pushkin Russian Language Institute in Moscow in the late 1980s, and he worked as a translator in the Moscow CNN office. He also worked on Soviet fishing boats in the Bering Sea for six months.

Acknowledgments

My wife, Deanna, and children, Alex and Elizabeth, allowed me a few moments of peace and quiet to write this book. I am grateful to Charles Cavaliere and Al Andrea for their encouragement and support. The critical comments of the anonymous readers were incisive and constructive.

My colleagues Marie Kelleher, Lise Sedrez, Ali Igmen, Hugh Wilford, and Ken Curtis at the history department of California State University, Long Beach, offered excellent comments during a 2008 presentation of this material. Arnie Kaminsky provided background on Indian history and contacts for my research trip to the city. The Yadunandan Center for India Studies at California State University, Long Beach, funded my trip to Bhopal in the summer of 2008. Deipica Bagchi arranged for interviews with Bhopal victims and was a gracious host during my stay in Bhopal.

My Russian colleague, Vitaliy Bezrogov, supplied information about Russian history textbook coverage of Chernobyl. Robert Kane at Niagara University suggested that I consider Minamata as a case study. The archivists at the New York State Archives in Albany, NY, the Niagara Falls Public Library in Niagara Falls, NY, and the University of Buffalo were professional and courteous. My students at California State University, Long Beach, have read or heard many versions of these chapters and their comments and criticisms were essential. Any problem with the book's content, of course, is entirely my doing.

Introduction

Governments and corporations across the globe have invariably promised that megaprojects to transform nature—nuclear power plants, chemical factories, and massive dams—would make the world a better place. The reality, however, has proved more complex. In the practice of large-scale technological development, results often differ radically from anticipated outcomes. While technology and economic development have undoubtedly produced jobs, raised standards of living, and simplified many aspects of daily life, they have also been accompanied by greed, corruption, and pollution. Leaders in Asia, Africa, Europe, and the Americas have used technology as a means of economic development—and as an instrument of oppression. Industrial managers have characterized machines that replace jobs and generate profits for a privileged few as a net gain for society and economic efficiency, a debatable proposition in many instances. New national elites in India, Brazil, Japan, and elsewhere used successful industrialization to defend their power and privilege. Even the pollution that came from new industries, they opined, smelled like progress, so they urged their citizens to get used to it because, in the end, pollution was really just a sign of a vibrant economy and brighter future. As the Brazilian president Jose Sarney once remarked, "Let pollution come, as long as factories come with it."

Politics, power, society, and technological development are thus inextricably intertwined in modern world history. Given this intricate matrix of connections, spectacular technological failure is bound to have momentous political and social consequences. What happens when the instruments of progress turn into exploding nuclear reactors, killer clouds of toxic chemicals, and toxic waste dumps filled with deadly carcinogens? At what point do societies realize that pollution no longer smells like progress but is really just pollution and might even kill you? Is progress to die for?

MODERNITY'S POLLUTION PROBLEMS

Technological development involves a complex series of trade-offs between economic development and environmental degradation. By some estimates, 3 billion people live in cities whose air is unfit to breathe. In the United States alone, the world's richest nation, more than 10 million people live within 1 mile of a federally recognized toxic waste site. More than 1,000 such "Superfund" sites in the United States have yet to be properly cleaned. Those toxic waste dumps are the price tag of economic power, though few calculate dioxin-laden landfills into the balance sheet of progress. Meanwhile, Chinese officials recently noticed an alarming rise in birth defects: a 40 percent increase during 2001–2006, which follows more or less the same trajectory as the nation's explosive economic growth. A dramatic increase in coal-fired energy plants has thus fueled China's economic miracle, along with severe health problems directly linked to coal-plant emissions.[1] Far from being a relic of the early years of the industrial revolution, mining and burning coal has increased 500-fold since the supposedly dirty old days of industrialization in early 1800s England.

---

[1]*Los Angeles Times*, February 2, 2009, A6.

While the evidence is overwhelming that technological and scientific progress has caused human and environmental damage, few textbooks of modern world history focus on the costs of development. According to the narrative of progress taught in most places around the world, technology fixes problems rather than creates them. Outside of environmental activists or a small group of academic specialists, the history of technology and science in the modern world remains, by and large, a story of relentless forward movement toward a better and safer world. To the extent that technological and environmental disasters enter the story, they do so as exceptional events, as temporary setbacks rather than regular features of modern life.

One of the bigger points to emerge in the chapters that follow is that large-scale technological failures, far from being exceptional, are normal in modern world history. Seen in a world historical rather than narrowly national context, technological disasters happen with astonishing frequency—regardless of political system, cultural context, and level of economic development. In the words of one influential sociologist in disaster studies, large-scale technological disasters are "normal accidents," inevitable products of the interaction of flawed human beings with incredibly complex and dangerous technological and scientific processes. Just like pollution, toxic waste disasters were a result of progress rather than its antithesis. So why are societies so often incapable of seeing this connection?

This book focuses on the costs of progress, not to suggest that industrial progress has been all for naught but to insert the often overlooked costs of modern industrial and urban development back into the story of modern world history. It uses four case studies to examine the political, social, and ecological fallout of technological and toxic waste disasters in the twentieth century: the mass mercury poisoning of Japanese fishermen in Minamata, Japan, after World War II; the Love Canal chemical dump that devastated the community of Niagara Falls in the United States in the 1970s; a colossal chemical leak in the Indian city of Bhopal in December 1984; and the explosion of a nuclear reactor at Chernobyl in the former Soviet Union in 1986. While each of these disasters is associated with a specific year or decade, from the 1950s to the 1980s, the factors that caused these disasters and their aftermath span a much longer time period and encompass the entire twentieth century.

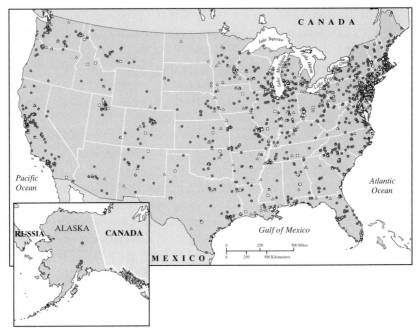

MAP I.1 Superfund is the federal government's program to clean up hazardous waste sites

Note: The fund to identify and manage waste sites—funded by taxpayers and contributions from polluters—was created in response to Love Canal. In 2008, the U.S. Environmental Protection Agency managed 1255 sites as a "national priority" and identified 63 new sites. "Deleted" sites (indicated on the map by triangles) are those waste dumps which have been declared clean.

METHODOLOGY

Although some historians look at monuments of culture and faith to understand a society, this book attempts to comprehend a society by looking at its monuments of filth, its industrial wastes. Though often unacknowledged, the more a society developed, the more it produced lethal toxic wastes. The four case studies represent a kind of archaeological dig, examining how four seemingly distinct societies handled their most toxic industrial excrement. The management of toxic wastes in each case study—where they were dumped, who had the misfortune of living by them, and especially what happened when they leaked or exploded—may reveal as much or more about a society than the more conventional materials of historical study, such as political elections or military conflicts. As you read the case studies, consider how industrial waste management practices—and the social, cultural, and political values revealed by those practices—not only connected the four societies under examination but also distinguished them on the stage of world history.

THE FOUR HORSEMEN OF THE TOXIC APOCALYPSE

Beginning in the 1930s, the Chisso Corporation, one of Japan's largest chemical companies, began dumping mercury-laced water directly into the Minamata Bay in Japan. The fishermen who lived off the catch from the bay, as well as those who consumed the bay's fish, began suffering severe symptoms of mercury poisoning. Yet for decades, government and corporate officials denied that Chisso had anything to do with their illness, dubbed "Minamata disease" in the Japanese press in the late 1950s. While Minamata was not unique in the world—there have been many other instances of mass mercury poisoning—it was the first such poisoning to draw widespread worldwide attention in the late 1950s and 1960s. The tragedy continued to draw attention into the mid-1970s, as victims' groups struggled with corporate and government officials to secure justice and compensation. For many individuals around the world, Minamata was the proverbial canary in the coal mine of modernity, the terrifying dark side of petrochemical industrialization. Among other things, in response to Minamata, consumer advocates in the United States launched a campaign to check all seafood for mercury contamination. They discovered, much to their chagrin, that much of what they ate also contained deadly mercury.

Love Canal in the late 1970s was the next "Minamata" in modern world history. Like Minamata, a powerful and nationally respected petrochemical corporation had poisoned the community of Love Canal with the indiscriminate dumping of lethal chemicals. Love Canal was the quintessential baby-boom suburb, located on the American side of the famous Niagara Falls in the industrial city of Niagara Falls, New York. Unbeknownst to its residents, however, the community in the 1950s was built on top of a chemical waste dump that had been covered with dirt and sold to real-estate developers by the Hooker Chemical Corporation (now Occidental Petroleum). As with Minamata, the community of Love Canal experienced a slow, invisible toxic immersion. At first, Love Canal residents thought they were living the suburban American dream. By the mid-1970s, as residents began suffering from a disturbing combination of ailments and diseases, the American dream had turned into a nightmare—a three-bedroom, two-car garage on top of a big pile of dioxin (one of many extremely carcinogenic substances buried beneath the new suburb of Love Canal). Only after years of legal struggle and political controversy did the polluters and the state act to protect citizens; but even then, many believed the process of remediation was far from complete and justice far from served.

Like an award ceremony in some macabre competition, the title of toxic waste disaster of the century passed in December 1984 from Love Canal to Bhopal, India. In contrast to Love Canal or Minamata, death in the central Indian city of Bhopal did not come slowly over the course of decades, but in the form of a massive cloud of leaked toxic gas from a Union Carbide plant. The cloud descended upon the slums adjacent to the factory, killing nearly 5,000 people instantly and permanently disabling tens of thousands. Bhopal became the world's poster child of technological and environmental disasters. Instead of speaking of the next "Minamata" or "Love Canal," people wondered when and how the next "Bhopal" would strike.

With each disaster, the threads linking seemingly distinct societies and communities around the globe became more apparent, a harbinger of what people today call "globalization." Following the Bhopal disaster, the *New York Times* contemplated the connections between Bhopal, the United States, and Japan. The "paper of record," as it used to be known before the age of the Internet, remembered a heretofore obscure instance of chemical poisoning when, "between 400 and 5,000 Iraqis died after consuming mercury-treated grain imported from the U.S."[2] Undoubtedly, the post–World War II period was a time of unprecedented growth and peace, but Japanese fishermen in Minamata, slum dwellers of Bhopal, and Iraqi consumers of American grain also realized, at least for a time, that the fruits of progress could be tainted by chemical poisons.

Just as people had become accustomed to thinking of Bhopal as the template for toxic terror, one of four reactors at a nuclear power plant in Chernobyl exploded on April 26, 1986. The explosion of the nuclear power plant in the Soviet Union immediately pushed Bhopal to the B and C sections of the world's newspapers, a shift that disappointed many Bhopal victims and activists who had counted on

---

[2]"Corporations Forced to Reassess Risks and to Review Safety Rules," *New York Times*, December 16, 1984, A1.

worldwide publicity to help them press their legal claims. While the explosion of the power plant at Chernobyl created a massive zone of contaminated air and land, from Ukraine and Belarus to Sweden and Finland, it also played no small role in the complete collapse of the Soviet Union in 1991, which was totally unprepared to deal with the political as well as radiological fallout of the disaster. So here they are, the four horsemen of the toxic apocalypse: Minamata, Love Canal, Bhopal, and Chernobyl. For a time, they united much of the twentieth-century world into one global community of fear and panic. Communities otherwise divided by culture, tradition, and political ideology discovered in each disaster a common global frame of reference: a shared experience of suffering and victimization.

COMMON THEMES TO CONSIDER

National boundaries are marked by steel fences, entry points, cement walls, and precise lines on a map. Yet those boundaries are far more ambiguous than the maps suggest. When environmental disaster strikes, pollution does not stop at the border. Radiation from Chernobyl, for example, blew northwest and irradiated much of Belarus and even parts of Scandinavia. "The Chernobyl disaster taught us there are no borders to the modern world," said the chief Belarus official responsible for dealing with the aftermath of Chernobyl in a 1996 interview with the *New York Times*. "It taught us to question faith in technology and in ourselves."[3] Similar tales of porous boundaries appear in each of the case studies. Although the disasters happened in a particular national context, their origins and consequences were supranational; they required global legal and political responses that severely strained the twentieth-century division of the world into supposedly sovereign nation-states. One of the aims of this book is to flesh out the inherent tension between a global society based on nation-states and the processes of global development that transcend national boundaries. Those tensions constituted a central dynamic around which world history has and will continue to develop.

The doctrine of progress also looms large in all four case studies. Occidental or oriental, capitalist or communist, first or third world, all

---

[3]"10 Years Later, Through Fear, Chernobyl Still Kills in Belarus," *New York Times*, March 31, 1996, A1.

four societies in these case studies shared an abiding faith in the doctrine of progress. Just like pollution, that doctrine transcended economic, political, and cultural differences, creating a kind of metaideology of global development. At the most basic level, the idea of progress is the belief that tomorrow (usually measured in terms of economic output and standard of living) will be better than today. Getting to that better world, however, always turned out to be more complex that people originally imagined. The unanticipated route to a better future, an illustration of the law of unintended consequences, is one of the perils of progress. People in Minamata, Love Canal, Bhopal, and Chernobyl imagined that they were going to one agreeable place; decades later they ended up somewhere else that was completely and shockingly different. Did the trauma of that realization force these societies to recalculate the pluses and minuses of technological development—and if so, how?

THE BLAME GAME

When progress went horribly wrong, people understandably looked for someone to blame, as if the ritual of arresting and punishing would put society back on the anticipated path. The search for the guilty party, however, almost always glossed over the complex motives of those who created the technologies that went awry. What distinguishes toxic waste disasters from the Nazi death camps or Saddam Hussein's use of chemical weapons on his own people is that the organizers of the technological disasters discussed in this book did not intend to cause harm. On the contrary, they saw themselves as a positive and humane force in history, even as heroes. In the Soviet Union of the 1960s and 1970s, two brothers authored a series of extremely popular science fiction novels centered around a group of "progressors."[4] These "progressors," similar to the government, industrial, and scientific leaders mentioned in this book's case studies, traveled the universe to bring the blessings of science and technology to various life forms and humanoids. The novels are essentially a retelling of the ancient Greek myth of Prometheus. The myth comes in two versions. In one, Prometheus, one of the Titans,

---

[4]The two brothers, Arkady and Boris Strugatsky, had one of their most popular science fiction novels translated and published in English in 1977 under the title *Roadside Picnic*.

steals the secret of fire from the gods to benefit humanity. He is punished for his act of thievery by being chained to a rock and having his liver pecked out daily by a bird of prey, only to have it regenerated each night, so that the torture could continue into eternity. Another version, however, presents Prometheus as someone who wants the secrets of the gods for purely selfish motives: to fashion a being from clay. In the first case, Prometheus, the "progressor," is motivated by altruism, a desire to help humanity by exploiting the "secrets" of nature. In the second case, Prometheus is motivated by vanity and a hunger for power and dominion over other people as his creation. The "progressors" in all the case studies of this book, like Prometheus, are a composite of both attributes, a combination of selfishness and selflessness. Each of the large-scale technological enterprises emerged from a complex mix of altruism and greed. It is therefore important to avoid simplistic explanations that attribute these disasters exclusively to corporate greed, a lust for power, or some other selfish intent. The truth was more complex than that—and more interesting.

While hindsight allows the historian to develop a more balanced assessment of motives and causes, it was extremely difficult for societies in all four case studies to be so balanced. People, especially victims and their relatives, wanted crystal clear villains and heroes, martyrs and saints. When the Union Carbide plant exploded in Bhopal, Indian journalists immediately called the accident a "holocaust," a deliberate attempt to equate the Bhopal leak with the Nazi death camps. The term screamed out from newspaper headlines, political pamphlets, and political speeches. The American chief executive officer (CEO) of the company, Warren Anderson, was represented in the Indian press as a war criminal, a Hitler. Some Indian journalists and politicians created the story that the accident was the product of a Pentagon chemical weapons experiment on the impoverished Indian masses, a view (not supported by a shred of historical evidence) still held by many in Bhopal in the summer of 2008. The idea of the Bhopal disaster as a holocaust is a powerful and moving image, one that captures the outrage of Bhopal victims and residents. But from a historian's point of view, the metaphor of Bhopal as a holocaust is completely wrong. There was no intent to kill in Bhopal. The absence of evil intent makes the disaster very different from the industrialized killing in the Nazi death camps. In legal terminology, Bhopal was negligent manslaughter, perhaps, but not murder.

Rather than a homicidal maniac, a mass murderer on a par with Hitler, Warren Anderson was the bespectacled, unremarkable CEO of a company trying to make money, provide jobs for Indians, and produce chemical fertilizers that might improve Indian agricultural yields. He gave speeches to fraternal lodges about the blessings of the chemical revolution and progress in general for mankind. Mass death at the plant in far-away Bhopal was an unintended consequence, paradoxically, of his attempt, vaguely conceived, to realize a conception of progress based on building chemical factories to produce chemical fertilizers, which in turn would hopefully improve agricultural productivity and end famine in the "third world." That the company and its shareholders would also profit was part of a win-win scenario that the Union Carbide CEO never doubted until it was too late. Given the scale of suffering at Bhopal, as in all the other case studies of this book, it is hard for people to accept that their suffering might have resulted from the likes of Warren Anderson. If the disasters discussed in this book represent evil, it is inadvertent and unintended evil.

CONSPIRACY THEORY AND HISTORICAL AMNESIA

In most of the case studies of this book, the inability to confront the "inadvertent" nature of the disasters had two important results. Victims, lawyers, journalists, and politicians invariably created a story of the disaster that identified clear villains (evil corporations, foreign enemies, saboteurs inside the factory) who caused and profited from the disaster. Identifying particular people responsible for the disaster provided the comforting story that the accident was caused by a human being out of control rather than a system or technology out of control. Journalists and politicians repeated and elaborated those stories of conspiracy and evil-doing, which often came to dominate society's memory of the events. The simplistic explanations offered to the public, however, differed from historical truth, which was almost always more complex and morally ambiguous.

Historical amnesia represented another powerful response to the incomprehensibility of inadvertent evil. In all four case studies, there was a striking contrast between an initial burst of intense media attention and coverage of these disasters and the tendency, decades later, for people to forget that they had ever happened. The absence of historical memory partly results from an understandable human desire to avoid thinking about unpleasant things that do not easily fit into prevailing conceptions of how the world works. But the process of forgetting was also aided and abetted by state institutions, especially state-funded systems of education. The exclusion of these disasters from publicly funded educational curricula in most of the societies discussed in this book illustrates how difficult it is to incorporate topics considered important by professional historians into public systems of education, especially when those stories contradict the triumphant story of progress preferred by most politicians and even average citizens.

THE MORAL DIMENSION

Finally, all of the societies in this study had difficulty relating scientific and technological progress to moral and ethical development. As in Mary Shelley's classic 1818 novel *Frankenstein: A Modern Day Prometheus*, in which Dr. Frankenstein gives no thought to the possible consequences of creating a new form of life, hardly anyone involved in the disasters of this book spent much time thinking about the ethical and moral implications of their actions. They were in too much of hurry. Whether in Niagara Falls or Bhopal, Minamata or Chernobyl, technological and scientific capabilities had far outstripped moral capabilities. The complex, hierarchical systems responsible for the disasters encouraged this disconnect. Workers simply did what they were told, assuming that the people who told them to bury the toxic wastes, or build a house on top of it, or dump the mercury-laced water into the water knew what they were doing. They didn't think about the consequences of their actions because they assumed someone with more responsibility, and higher up the chain of corporate or government command, had done the thinking for them. But they had not. The abdication of thought and responsibility went all the way to the top. A *New York Times* article, entitled "The Pain of Progress," remarked, "[G]iven the fact that we are synthesizing substances of unbelievable lethal quality, we must ask ourselves whether we have the management capability to deal with them."[5]

If the creators of these technologies often had moral blind spots, others also suffered from moral lapses. While no one wanted these

---

[5]"The Pain of Progress Racks the Third World," *New York Times*, December 9, 1984. E4.

disasters to happen, there were many people who benefited from them in various perverse and sometimes unexpected ways. An army of American tort lawyers followed immediately in the wake of the chemical leak in Bhopal, the "great ambulance chase," as one newspaper termed it. Dozens of American lawyers roamed the streets of Bhopal, signing up victims. Ultimately, more than 1 million people applied for compensation as victims of Bhopal, even though the entire population of the city was just 800,000 at the time! The lawyers were joined by the "peddlers of the apocalypse," as one Chernobyl victim put it: the journalists, environmental activists, radical politicians, and many others who treated the disasters as signs of the imminent collapse of civilization and as proof of a need for radical change. Some, of course, just wanted to sell newspapers and books filled with titillating details, a pornography of pain and suffering for various literate publics. Others used images, often far more effectively than scientific data, to propagandize the suffering of the victims and to sway public and political opinion. In each of the case studies, the public "consumed" the disasters in various newspapers and magazines along with gruesome and macabre images of deformed and damaged bodies, a freak show that often had the unintended consequence of turning all victims, in the eyes of surrounding society, into freaks. Tour companies—often carrying busloads of Japanese tourists—began toxic tours of Love Canal during the 1980s. Tourists would stare at Love Canal residents as if they were zoo animals. Tour companies also began offering tours of the Chernobyl zone. The point is not to minimize the suffering in all of these disasters, but to note the tendency among certain groups to exaggerate and exploit suffering and damage—just as it was in the interest of others to minimize the suffering that their technological systems had caused.

In the end, each of these disasters revealed that most people had far less control over their own lives than they had assumed. The realization struck at the heart of a central promise of the scientific and technological revolutions and attacked the doctrine of progress that had driven much of global development in the twentieth century. Far from making life more secure, science and technology had in fact created a profound sense of insecurity. Before the modern era the most lethal disasters came from nature; in the age of science and technology they were often unintended products of human artifice.

The Minamata Disaster and the True Costs of Japanese Modernization

In 1900, Minamata Bay was a sleepy fishing village, located on the west coast of the Japanese island of Kyushu about 560 miles southwest of Tokyo. The bay was nature's bounty. The ocean served up a rich variety of seafood, and its tidal shallows were a veritable sea garden filled with clams, oysters, and sea cucumbers. The rituals and rhythms of fishing—the building of small boats and weaving of nets, and the predawn venture out to sea and arrival back at the docks at dusk—created a community based on an intensely intimate relationship with the natural world. It was a low-tech venture: mostly wood and thread spun, shaped, and hewed into various fishing implements. Identity in the fishing community of Minamata emerged from labor in the natural world and from working with natural materials to harvest the waters. Life was hard and poverty endemic, to be sure, but the waters, at least, provided a livelihood and a way of life.

CHISSO CORPORATION

However, a newer community soon came to Minamata, an industrial community funded and employed by the Chisso Corporation. The chemical giant was founded as an electric power company in 1906 by an electrical engineering graduate of Tokyo University—Japan's Harvard. To use surplus energy, the company in 1907 and 1908 built a chemical fertilizer plant in the coastal town of Minamata. The drama and unexpected turns of Japanese modernization are written into the history of this corporation, as Japan competed with Europeans and Americans at their own game of modernization with the help of businesses such as Chisso. Initially, the company produced hydro-electric power to compensate for the nation's lack of oil and other energy sources. In the 1920s and 1930s, as Japan sought to establish its dominance in East Asia, the company dramatically expanded the production of chemical fertilizers to maximize agricultural production on Japan's scarce land resources.

Eager to avoid the fate of China, whose economic underdevelopment made the country easy prey for American and European interests, Japanese leaders married capitalist industrial progress to the authoritarian structures of traditional Japanese society. Individuals were expected to bow down before corporate and state authority, enduring hardship and sacrifice for the sake of Japanese industrial might. That was especially true in the 1930s. In 1932, Chisso began producing acetaldehyde, a chemical used to manufacture drugs, plastics, and an array of industrial products, many of them critical for fulfilling Japan's own imperial ambitions in East Asia. The company used inorganic mercury as a chemical catalyst, producing methyl mercury as a waste by-product, which it dumped directly into the bay until 1968.

Like the mythological phoenix rising from the ashes, Chisso stepped up production following World War II, determined to build a chemical future on the ruins of devastating defeat. The humiliation and devastation of defeat in World War II—culminating in the bomb-ings of Hiroshima and Nagasaki—intensified the desire among Japanese politicians and citizens to rebuild and modernize after the war. Chisso, like Japan more generally, boomed during the 1950s, coupling Minamata to the bullet train of Japan's post–World War II economic miracle. The industrial jobs provided by Chisso marked the transformation of Minamata from a supposedly "backward" agrarian and fishing community to a modern industrial society. Alongside the traditional fishing community of Minamata, whose waters were increasingly fouled, Chisso had created a factory town.

Lingering feudal structures and attitudes reinforced Chisso's authority and power in Minamata. White-collar Chisso executives lived in the center of the town, occupied in feudal times by the

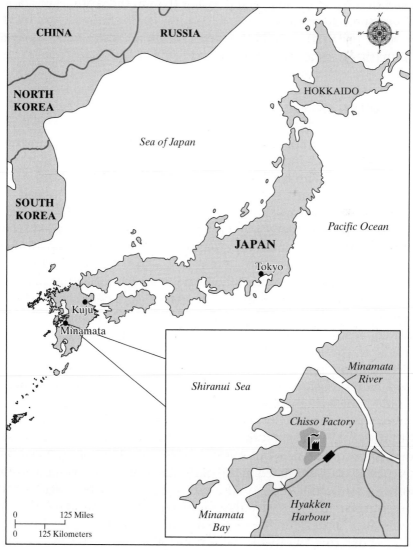

MAP 1.1   Japan and surrounding countries, with an inset showing Minamata

daimyo, or lord, and his samurai retainers. The 5,000 or so workers employed by Chisso (and the families and subsidiary businesses that relied on their salaries) depended on an industrial process that dumped tons of mercury-laced treatment water into the bay. Moreover, their relationship to Chisso management and its industrial processes defined their individual and community identities. Unlike many of the fishermen, Chisso worker identities and livelihoods were rooted in the factory compound rather than in the natural world. Put starkly, their survival seemed to require (though they were hardly aware of it at first) the end to fishing in Minamata—and to the community that had depended upon it.

DISTURBING SIGNS

The devastation of the fishing community of Minamata was, in effect, the bill of Japanese industrialization come due. It was a familiar story, whereby those who bore the costs of industrialization were not its primary beneficiaries. In 1953, Minamata residents first noticed that cats and dogs fed fish scraps from the docks of Minamata Bay began to suffer from strange convulsions and bizarre behavior—dancing wildly, tearing at themselves, foaming at the mouth, and flinging themselves into the ocean to die. Crows crashed wildly into the rocks and dropped dead from the sky. Residents began to suffer alarming symptoms, including uncontrollable tremors and convulsions, loss of speech and hearing, and numbness. Those symptoms, it was later learned, resulted from methyl mercury compounds, which were present in the local daily diet of contaminated seafood, that had penetrated the nervous system. They were the classic symptoms of "mad-hatter disease," the name derived from an earlier instance of mercury poisoning in the nineteenth century that afflicted English hatters who worked with mercury-treated felt and fur. In the case of the Minamata residents, the mercury transformed brain cells and other areas of the nervous system into a black, spongy mass. The mercury also accumulated in the placenta of pregnant women, giving fetuses a concentrated dose. Affected children were born with conditions similar to cerebral palsy, only with permanently deformed brains and limited intelligence. Kazumitsu Hannaga was one such child—born to a paralyzed father and abandoned by his shocked mother in 1955. He spent most of his life in a hospital, his head tilted to one side and his deformed, spindly legs curled up under his wheel chair. In 1956, the Japanese medical community and media coined the phrase "Minamata disease" to describe his condition, but its cause was still a mystery. Some thought it was contagious, so they placed victims in isolated wards and insane asylums.

While the medical experts pleaded ignorance, many locals believed that Chisso had something to do with their condition. The fishermen, for instance, noticed that the fish near the Chisso pipes floated dead on top of the water. They began petitioning local authorities for help in the late 1950s. Numerous political and cultural factors, however, stood in the way of the Minamata activists, who struggled mightily for nearly two decades before corporate and state officials acknowledged the true source of their misery.

POLITICAL AND CULTURAL OBSTACLES

Under American occupation, the Japanese awoke in the new year of 1947 and discovered that they had been transformed from subjects with limited rights to citizens of a constitutional democracy. However, democratic institutions rarely emerge so quickly, especially at the end of a bayonet (or in Japan's case, amidst the radioactive fallout of two atomic bombs). Compared to the United States, the Japanese had a weak tradition of community activism and local democracy, hardly fertile ground for the imposition of a new constitutional order by outside American occupiers. Since the Meiji Restoration of 1867, which initiated a period of intense modernization under the Japanese emperor, newspapers, schools, government officials, and corporate leaders had inculcated in the country's inhabitants a belief that industrialization and individual sacrifice were essential to Japan's survival as a nation—and to its ability to fend off Western industrial powers. Individuals were treated more as subjects with duties and obligations and less as citizens with inalienable rights.

The spirit of individual and communal sacrifice carried over into the post–World War II period, creating an extremely hostile environment for grassroots activism—especially when directed against as powerful a force in local and national politics as the Chisso Corporation. While the Chisso Corporation provided jobs, for politicians it was the feeding hand that no one dared to bite. Using the company's charitable donations and taxes, the regional government, known in

Japan as a "prefecture," built and operated schools and hospitals. Moreover, according to the dominant value system of Japan's modernizers, the supposedly traditional and "backward" Minamata fishermen were destined to disappear. They were relics of the past, in stark contrast to the Chisso Corporation, which politicians and journalists continued to glorify after the war as an agent of national progress.

Challenging Chisso was therefore akin to challenging Japanese progress—a quixotic, seemingly insane, and antisocial endeavor from the perspective of most Japanese. Even conceptions of "pollution" in Japanese culture worked against the victims (though this was hardly unique to Japan, as the other case studies illustrate). The Japanese word for pollution, *kogai*, means "public nuisance," something that destroys a harmonious civic life. Pollution can, therefore, be social or physical, a challenge to the social status quo or an actual physical threat to the community's health. In the Japanese cultural context, those who talked about pollution and demanded justice could therefore be seen as the most dangerous polluters, since their complaints threatened and disturbed the existing order.

The fishermen also had practical economic reasons to keep their condition private. To speak of the disease, should it be linked to the fish they ate would destroy their livelihood. Besides, others within the fishing community no doubt had relatives and friends who worked in the factory. Many fishermen, moreover, were ashamed of their physical weakness and afraid that talking about it would lead to ostracism for themselves and their families. As in most societies of the 1950s, including the United States, physically deformed and mentally impaired people were hidden away—put in asylums or otherwise shut behind closed doors. The socially accepted response to pollution and extreme physical suffering was silence, not public questioning. The ailing fishermen and their families discovered they were no good for Minamata, even (and most damningly) in their own view of themselves.

LIFTING THE VEIL OF SILENCE

Ultimately, the authority of scientific research and expertise helped to lift the veil of silence and shame. Of all things, a Chisso employee, a conscientious medical doctor named Dr. Hajime Hosokawa, conducted the critical piece of research that proved Chisso was the source of Minamata disease. In the late 1950s, Hosokawa tested waste water from Chisso's pipes on cats, demonstrating to his own great dismay that it produced all the symptoms of Minamata disease. In 1957, scientists from Kumamoto University, working with Dr. Hosokawa, released a study arguing that the victims became sick due to ingesting heavy metals in fish caught from Minamata Bay. In 1959 they confidently affirmed that Chisso was the source of the mercury. The story at this point took a turn characteristic of all the case studies of this book. Dr. Hosokawa faced intense pressure from his employer to end his investigation. While Chisso denied all claims that it was the source of contamination, the Japan Chemical Industry Association in 1959 produced a report claiming the disease could not possibly be linked with mercury. The Japanese Ministry of International Trade and Industry— whose mandate was industrial development and not environmental protection—suspended all ongoing government scientific studies on Minamata.

In 1959, 4,000 outraged fishermen demanded an audience with Chisso management, which had offered them small "sympathy" payments to compensate them for dirtying their waters. Angrily rejecting the adequacy of the proposed payments, they stormed the factory compound, an action that threatened to shut down its operations and put thousands of employees out of work. As Chisso dug in its heels and refused to offer more money or admit any guilt, the fishermen issued forth a barrage of petitions to politicians at all levels, gradually abandoning the tone of humble supplication present in their first petitions. They picketed the company headquarters and operations. They gave interviews with newspapers and choreographed demonstrations to maximize negative publicity for Chisso, hoping to shame the corporation into further action.

The militancy of the fishermen in 1959 turned out to be a tactical mistake, a step ahead of the more radical politics of the late 1960s. Instead of compensation and medical help, the Minamata activists received a sobering lesson in the limits of Japan's postwar democracy. Local politicians uniformly sided with Chisso, condemning the fishermen. Local authorities, with some justice, feared that demands to change Chisso's production system would mean the loss of jobs and taxes. Chisso, meanwhile, shrewdly framed the conflict in terms of jobs, pitting workers of the factories—the "future" of Minamata— against the livelihood of the fishermen, supposedly Minamata's backward past. Industrial workers and their families dutifully joined the chorus of condemnation, attacking the fishermen's demands. A coalition of local labor unions held a press conference to denounce the company critics. Residents shunned the fishermen, treating them like lepers. Shop owners refused to serve them, and when they did they often demanded that money be left on the floor, which the proprietor would pick up disdainfully with chop sticks.

The political winds in 1959 were clearly blowing against the fishermen. In December 1959, following the public backlash against the activists, Chisso reduced its offer of "sympathy" payments to the victims to one-tenth the original offer. It also made recipients pledge to end all future protests or legal actions against the company and acknowledge that the company had nothing to do with their illness. The timing was intentional. Bills came due at the end of the year, so victims and their families were under intense pressure to pay off mounting debts from fishing and medical treatment. In the meantime, Chisso continued dumping mercury directly into the bay.

Adding insult to injury, news of the controversy destroyed the market for Minamata's fish. The governor of the local prefecture imposed a ban on the sale of fish from the bay, curiously, while simultaneously supporting the official Chisso position that there was no contamination problem. From the perspective of 1960, following Chisso's "resettlement" with the fishermen, it appeared as if the victims had suffered a humiliating defeat. Advancing Japan's national economic interests still seemed to require the poisoning of the environment—and the destruction of the livelihood and health of those who depended upon it.

THE BATTLE REJOINED

Just as the Minamata controversy seemed to be fading from public memory, a new outbreak of a similar disease occurred in Niigata in 1965, another prefecture of Japan. A researcher at Niigata University began investigating the latest outbreak of what the medical textbooks now called "Minamata disease," this time caused by another company. Breaking his company-enforced silence, Dr. Hosokawa, the Chisso Corporation physician whose earlier research had shown a link between mercury dumping and the disease, joined the team of researchers in Niigata.

On June 12, 1967, thirteen victims in Niigata were persuaded by maverick lawyers and activists (despite harassment by corporate thugs) to file Japan's first pollution lawsuit. The breakthrough in the trial came when Dr. Hosokawa testified about his earlier experiments reproducing the symptoms of the Minamata disease in lab animals. His evidence turned the tide of the Niigata case, and the government finally acknowledged in 1968 that mercury dumping had been a probable (though not definitive) cause of the disease suffered in Niigata. While not implicated in the decision, Chisso understood its potential liability and immediately stopped pouring mercury into Minamata Bay, more than 35 years after it began the dumping.

Emboldened by the example of the Niigata victims, 112 patients from 39 families in Minamata filed a lawsuit against Chisso on June 14, 1969. At first, it seemed as if the outcome of the case would turn on scientific proof, as in the Niigata case. But the Chisso Corporation was determined to defend itself from any admission of criminal guilt and further compensation payments. Basing their conclusions on scientific studies funded by the government and the company, Chisso lawyers argued that the scientific evidence was "inconclusive." Even if industrial pollution had caused the disease, they said it was impossible to prove that Chisso's waste pipes were the source.

ATOMIC BOMBS, GODZILLA, AND THE CULTURE OF VICTIMIZATION

If the science involved in the issue proved indecisive and adaptable, the social and political climate in Japan, compared to the late 1950s, was far more favorable toward the Minamata victims. During the 1960s, Japanese political values had shifted rapidly with the rise of a new generation after World War II. The shift mirrored changes in much of the world in the 1960s. In the United States, for example, a new environmental consciousness emerged in response to books such as Rachel Carson's *Silent Spring*, published in 1962, a critical moment in drawing worldwide attention to the dangers of widespread chemical use. Inspired in part by American civil rights activists of the 1960s, Japanese citizens expressed a new willingness to confront corporate and political authorities, a willingness that reflected a desire to move away from pre–World War II authoritarianism and toward a more democratic, postwar order.

Many Japanese were also beginning to think of themselves as consumers and not just as producers. In contrast to the lean and desperate postwar years of the 1950s, people wanted to enjoy the Japanese economic miracle of the 1960s. Preparing, displaying, and consuming seafood in a myriad of forms became an essential part of modern Japanese identity and consumer culture. Fish had symbolic and cultural power and not simply a caloric value. The Minamata fishermen exploited that cultural value to draw attention to their plight. In July 1973, for example, the union of Minamata fishermen dumped 5 tons of fresh sardines at the main gate of Chisso in protest of the contamination of the seas from the company's drains. Such actions drove home the message to Japanese consumers that Minamata's plight affected them personally.

Finally, the Minamata victims skillfully turned their suffering from liability to asset. It was a strategy that many Japanese had used to deal with the humiliating defeat of World War II. Rather than seeing their nation as war criminal and aggressor in World War II, many Japanese redefined themselves as victims of American aggression. In shockingly lurid details, hundreds of documentaries, books, art exhibits, and newspaper accounts recounted the suffering of Hiroshima and Nagasaki. By the 1960s, these cultural productions legitimated public displays of victimization, physical suffering, and pain, thus transforming Japan from imperialist aggressor into victim of American militarism. Simultaneously, as in the United States of the 1960s, a counterculture began to question the costs of industrial development. Opponents of Japan's accelerated modernization criticized the pollution, pace, and sacrifices of modern industrial life. The movie monster Godzilla was the mutant, radioactive creature from the sea terrorizing the Japanese public with her toxic breath (the monster was a she). Godzilla, like the atomic bomb, presented the Japanese people as victims of modern science and industry, rather than its beneficiaries.

By the early 1970s, the Minamata activists struck a deep public chord, joining their cause to this growing culture of victimization. One victim, Michiko Ishimure, wrote a stirring account in 1970 of the Minamata tragedy, titled simply *Paradise of the Bitter Sea*. A shy, retiring housewife, Ishimure stepped out of the kitchen and into the public arena. Along the way she found a literary and political voice, an instance of women's empowerment replicated in the other case studies. Her book presented a powerful tale of the plight of the victims, combined with a nostalgic and lyrical description of the natural world and the human–nature relationship that Chisso had supposedly destroyed. It was both a milestone in Japanese literature and an inspiration for environmental activism in Japan.

Ishimure relied not on science to sway opinion, but on emotion and pathos, as did other activists. One 1971 documentary, entitled simply *Minamata*, combined a terse retelling of the facts of the case with painfully evocative images of mental impairment, paralysis, blindness, and death. The images, much more than the data, seemed to speak for themselves—and they told a story that always cast the Minamata victims in the role of heroic martyr and Chisso into the role of irredeemable villainy. After showing the suffering of the victims, the film climaxed with footage of a dramatic confrontation in 1970 between victims and the unsympathetic management of Chisso. A Tokyo lawyer counseled the victims to buy one share each of Chisso stock, which would give them the right to attend the company shareholders' meeting in Osaka. The victims, one-thousand strong, tapping into Buddhist customs, draped themselves in the white robes of pilgrims and recited Buddhist chants in unison. They rang small bells rhythmically, a symbolic call to the dead victims to join them in their fight. At the end of the meeting, the women among the victims rushed to the stage where Chisso's president sat. They raised memorial tables of deceased family members and implored the president to understand that Chisso's mercury had caused their suffering. The confrontation in 1970 was a dress rehearsal for a dramatic confrontation three years later that would mark another turning point in the struggle.

While the wheels of justice turned ever so slowly following the filing of the court case in 1969, a number of Minamata victims continued the tactic of directly confronting Chisso and government officials. As with the civil rights activists of the United States in the 1960s, the Minamata victims counted on persecution by Chisso to turn public opinion in their favor—and to shame corporate and government officials into action. They recognized a simple but powerful truth: Waiting for the lawyers and scientific experts to come to their rescue, as previous experience had shown, was a fool's errand. The system would not act on their behalf unless they forced it to do so.

SEEKING JUSTICE OUTSIDE THE COURTS

Teruo Kawamoto was one of the most militant of the activists. Born in 1931 to a fisherman, he was the eighth of 11 children, four of whom had died of malnutrition. He married in 1957 and almost immediately began to suffer from partial paralysis of his limbs and a stiffening of his tongue (relatively mild symptoms of Minamata disease). His father, however, suffered from acute symptoms of the disease and was completely bedridden. Duty-bound to the Confucian virtue of filial piety, a key element in Japanese culture, Kawamoto studied as an assistant nurse and took care of his father in a mental hospital as he died an agonizing and excruciatingly painful death. Thereafter, driven by grief and a sense of duty to his father, he devoted himself to finding and registering victims of Minamata disease. From 1971 to 1973, Kawamoto orchestrated sit-in campaigns. He set up a tent encampment outside the Chisso corporate headquarters. He worked with sympathetic journalists and environmental activists to publicize the Minamata case. After one skirmish with thugs from Chisso in 1972, the company sued him for assault, a case that Kawamoto won only after an eight-year legal battle decided by the Japanese Supreme Court.

Personally familiar with the halls of justice, Kawamoto believed the formal setting of a courtroom was devoid of emotion and tended to reinforce rather than challenge existing hierarchical relationships in society. He had learned firsthand the limited possibility of justice within the confines of a courtroom. Instead, he pushed for a face-to-face meeting with the president. Such a meeting would flatten the hierarchical arrangements of the courtroom and establish the relation between the company and victims as equals. It would also allow the victims to appeal to the emotions and feelings of the public rather than relying solely on the testimony of scientific experts, who always seemed to conclude that the data were "inconclusive."

Even when the Minamata victims who had sued Chisso in 1969 won their case in March 1973, Kawamoto was unimpressed and continued to demand an audience with the president of Chisso. Kawamoto, like many victims, demanded a public, personal apology from the president of Chisso and not merely financial compensation. "What we really wish to see," he said, "is the responsible people of the company becoming sensitized to those pains and sufferings of trees, fish, sea, and mountains, as well as us humans." A dramatic denouement came in August 1973, when Kawamoto and his group of patients finally received an audience with President Shimada of Chisso. A week's worth of tense negotiations ensued. At one point, Kawamoto asked Shimada if he was a religious man and if he prayed. Shimada admitted that he did and that he had a small room with a shrine on which the names of Minamata victims were inscribed. Nonetheless, Shimada told Kawamoto that the company could not provide the money that the victims wanted—it was simply too much. Suddenly, a victim arose, shaking violently. "I can't stand this any more! You can see for yourself. If I don't get the indemnity money, I can't live!" The victim grabbed a glass ashtray, broke it on the table, and slit his wrists with it. As blood spurted out, the shocked president muttered: "Yes, yes, yes—we will pay."[1]

And pay they did. In addition to making a formal personal apology to the victims, the president agreed to compensation of approximately $60,000 plus medical expenses to all victims and not just those who filed the suit. Chisso later paid compensation to various groups of fishermen across Japan whose livelihood, due to depressed demand for their catch, had been destroyed by the controversy. The financial strains of the case were so great that the Japanese government had to engineer a bailout for the Chisso Corporation in 1978—in part to ensure that Chisso, the main source of jobs for Minamata, would be able to continue paying compensation to victims.

As a result of the Minamata struggle, balancing environmental protection and economic growth had become a new political imperative. In March 1979, Japanese courts concluded the first criminal conviction for pollution, sentencing two Chisso executives to two years in prison. The determination to pursue polluters with criminal charges, combined with substantial awards to victims and costs for cleanup (totaling nearly $2 billion), stands in stark contrast to the other case studies in this book. In the end, nearly 2,250 patients were designated as victims.

THE UNIQUENESS OF THE JAPANESE CASE

A confluence of factors distinguished the Japanese case from the other case studies in this book. Corporate and government officials certainly used all available means to thwart charges made by victims and to

---

[1]Kazuko Tsurumi, *New Lives: Some Case Studies in Minamata* (Tokyo, Japan: Sophia University, 1988), 5–8; "The Dirty Hand of Industry in Southern Japan," *New York Times*, June 8, 1975, 249.

avoid paying for their polluting ways, a predictable response in almost every political and cultural context of the modern industrial era. But they were also remarkably susceptible to public shaming—in a way that could not be said, certainly, of Union Carbide officials in Bhopal or Hooker Chemical officials in Love Canal, as shown in the other case studies of this book. Japanese courts also showed a resolve and determination to punish corporations for criminal actions once they had become convinced that the corporations were responsible for the contamination. Images of Minamata's suffering, validated by the culture of victimization resulting from the bombs dropped on Hiroshima and Nagasaki, dominated the public understanding of the conflict. The Chisso Corporation was clearly identified in the court of public opinion, in addition to the legal system, as the victimizer—and the fishing community as victim.

While the Minamata activists skillfully presented their case to the public, the public by the early 1970s was also prepared to receive their message. Intense activism and press coverage on environmental issues had thrust the problem of pollution into the broader national conscious-ness by the late 1960s and onto the "to-do" lists of politicians. In 1967, as the Niigata victims filed their mercury poisoning lawsuit, Japan's national government created the "Basic Law for Environmental Pollu-tion Control." In 1970, an extraordinary session of the Japanese Diet passed a series of laws to regulate various types of pollution. Known as the "Pollution Diet," the legislature also made damaging human health with pollution a crime—the first nation to pass such a law.

The Minamata fishermen also benefited from a more general struggle to realize the promise of democratic control in the 1947 con-stitution. The environment was certainly important to many activists, but they also viewed environmental protection as a key test of Japan-ese democracy. Much like the issue of civil rights in the United States in the 1960s, environmental justice in Japan became a rallying call for those who pursued a broader agenda of democratization. In the end, the success of the Minamata victims reflected a more general transfor-mation of Japanese individuals from imperial subjects with limited rights to citizens of a constitutional democracy willing and able to confront powerful interests. Marking one significant point of that shift, in 1983 the activist Kawamoto was elected to the city council of Minamata, thus breaking the decades-long stranglehold over city politics by corporate and business interests. Minamata disease had ravaged Kawamoto's body, but it also gave him a political voice.

MINAMATA AS A GLOBAL EVENT

Although Minamata is often thought of as a Japanese tragedy, it also had global implications. Like Chernobyl and Bhopal, the disaster transcended national boundaries, illustrating the physical and imagined connections created by globalization. A Minamata victim and activist, Hamamoto Tsugunori was keenly aware of the tragedy's global significance. In 1972, he took his first trip abroad—to Stockholm to speak to a United Nations environmental conference about Minamata disease. He discovered that mercury poisoning was a global phenomenon. In 1975, he visited Canadian Indians suffering from mercury poisoning caused by a British multinational chemical corporation. He subsequently traveled throughout the world to speak of his experiences and to visit other sufferers of mercury poisoning. In the process, he helped to create a new community of victims that crossed national and ethnic boundaries.

Minamata was also well known in the United States, frequently appearing on the front page of newspapers such as the *New York Times* and *Los Angeles Times*. In response to Minamata, Americans at first gave themselves a pat on the back for being far better stewards of their environment than the Japanese, whose industrial successes in the 1970s had begun to eclipse those of the United States. But Americans soon discovered that they shared much more in common with the Japanese fishermen of Minamata than they had assumed. Consumer advocates in the United States, like their counterparts in Japan, began demanding testing for mercury in tuna and swordfish—and in fish from their own territorial waters. Recreational fishermen on Lake St. Clair in the United States and Canada were told they could no longer eat their catch when it was discovered that the waters had been poisoned by mercury. Commercial fisheries on Lake Ontario and the Niagara River were shut down after testing in the mid-1970s revealed high levels of mercury in fish and most have never been reopened. After news of Minamata, regulators of chemical industries in Niagara Falls in the 1970s—who had relied on "self-policing"—discovered that chemical companies were dumping mercury directly into the local waters that fed into Lake Ontario, the main source of drinking water for the Canadian city of Toronto across the border.

The more people around the world tested their food and water supplies for mercury, the more they realized that they, too, might suffer from Minamata disease, a universal rather than Japanese affliction. In

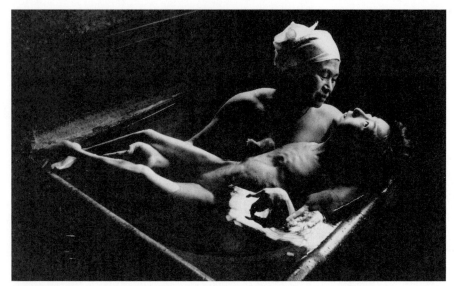

FIGURE 1.1   Minamata Tomoko is bathed by her mother. (Black Star)

1971, the U.S. Congress held a series of high-profile hearings on cases of mercury poisonings in the United States, an echo across the vast Pacific Ocean of the Minamata controversy. Another expert warned American dieters to limit their consumption of tuna fish sandwiches. More than one a day just might make them go Minamata.

THE APPEAL TO EMOTION

A far more cosmopolitan and integrated global media system also made Minamata a world event. Minamata, like the other tragedies in this book, became an event in modern world history because journalists, editors, and broadcasters paid attention to it. Americans, for example, took intense notice of Minamata in response to a series of photographic essays by the celebrated American photographer W. Eugene Smith. Smith was famous for his extended picture essays in *Life* magazine (then the most popular magazine in the country), including photographs of the bloody American taking of Iwo Jima from Japan during World War II. In 1971, Smith and his young wife of Japanese ancestry chronicled the struggles of the Minamata activists and victims. *Life*, in 1972, ran many of Smith's photos, which became an instant sensation. Smith displayed his images in dozens of magazines, newspapers, exhibits, and in his own book. One art critic described a famous portrait of a young victim, "her face and hands horribly distorted, being bathed by her mother, who gazes at her with gentle affection; both the pose and the mood of the picture recall the delicate sadness of Michelangelo's Pieta."[2] Smith called the picture "Tomoko in Her Bath," but it was known more widely as the "Minamata Pieta." It attained iconic status, subsequently featured in nearly every major newspaper and magazine article about the tragedy, including in Japan, where it fit in perfectly with the culture of victimization.

As in Japan, it was not the scientific evidence that swayed the American public of the mid-1970s, but the artistic presentation of the victims' suffering, referred to once by Smith as "industrial genocide." A *New York Times* reviewer noted in 1975: "[T]he details of an obscure provincial disaster took on the dimensions of high tragedy, and focused attention on the dangers of unrestrained industrialization in a way that no amount of dumb facts could." Smith, said the reviewer, had transformed the Minamata disease victims "into heroic saints and martyrs, and reduced the leaders and agents of a great industrial corporation to the level of villains." Soon, Americans would discover their own Minamata much closer to home in a place called Love Canal. It was a connection that many American consumers of Smith's Minamata imagery had not expected.[3]

A NEW WAY TO CALCULATE PROGRESS

While awakening many in Japanese society to the possibilities of grassroots activism, Minamata also helped to alter the way many Japanese defined progress. It was a commonplace in all modernizing societies that pollution is the price of progress. In response to Minamata, however, many Japanese adjusted their formula for the future by making a clean environment a precondition of progress. Progress, in other words, required protecting the environment rather than destroying it. It helped, of course, that Japan's economy had been growing at an annual rate of more than 15 percent in the

---

[2]"Re-evaluating the Work of W. Eugene Smith," *New York Times*, May 27, 1994, C24.
[3]"Minamata Victims Transformed," *New York Times*, May 11, 1975, D31.

1960s, making people believe that a clean environment was perhaps affordable. There is numerical evidence to support this shift in the Japanese conception of progress. Amidst the major pollution compensation trials of the early 1970s, in which Minamata figured prominently, public opinion polls consistently showed that large majorities of Japanese considered a clean environment more important than economic growth. According to national opinion polls in the period 1972–1975, Japanese citizens were willing to accept higher taxes in exchange for a cleaner environment. At least in part due to the Minamata controversy, Japan has taken a lead role in attempting to convince polluting countries to reduce greenhouse emissions. In 1997, Japan convened 160 nations in the city of Kyoto to set guidelines for reducing global emissions.

In June 2008, Shinto Ishihara, the flamboyant governor of the Tokyo region, broke ranks with the prime minister of Japan and decided to impose even more drastic reductions on greenhouse emissions in Japan's capital. Known for his right-wing nationalist views, including the hugely popular book of the 1980s entitled *The Japan that Can Say No*, Ishihara drew on his painful experiences as head of Japan's national environmental agency during the 1970s. At the time, he was at the epicenter of the Minamata mercury poisoning controversy and had supported Chisso. More than 30 years later, he cited the Minamata mercury poisoning as "the kind of tragedy that the government can cause when it fails to act." Ishihara said the main lesson he learned from the disaster was that, "when you try to catch up to developed countries, you end up ignoring environmental issues."[4]

Not only did Minamata cause many Japanese citizens, as well as politicians, to change their definition of "progress," it also allowed for the community to find a sense of closure conspicuously absent in the other case studies of this book. Various parts of Japanese society, including the legal system and public opinion, created a narrative about the tragedy that clearly identified victim and perpetrator. The Chisso Corporation's president, Kenichi Shamada, got down on his knees and apologized to the victims. It is hard to imagine the CEO of Hooker Chemical or Union Carbide, or the Soviet Union's Mikhail Gorbachev, prostrating themselves in such a fashion before victims, much less admitting any guilt for the disasters.

---

[4]"Tokyo Mayor Leads on Climate," *Financial Times*, June 3, 2008, 6.

A LINGERING TOXICITY

Still, despite the positive results, the tragic dimensions of Minamata should not be forgotten. While more than 2,000 survivors received generous compensation and medical care, 10,000 others were denied compensation on the grounds that they could not definitively prove that their illness was caused by Chisso. In 1996, as most of the uncompensated survivors were reaching the end of their lives, they finally gave up their struggle with Chisso and accepted payments of about $24,000, in exchange for dropping all further legal claims.

In the meantime, the polluted waters at Minamata retain their toxicity. Remediation, the technical term for cleaning up toxic wastes, meant building a 1.3 mile net in 1974 separating the bay from the open sea and dredging and burying on land the recovered, mercury-laced sediments of the bay's seabed. The stated purpose of the net, a sort of underwater fence, was to prevent the contaminated fish from traveling out of the bay, where they might be caught on the open seas by commercial fishing trawlers and consumed. But the real reason for the net had less to do with containing toxic wastes (engineers knew the net was no barrier for mercury-laced water and microbes) than with appeasing Japanese consumers, who feared that fish outside the bay were being contaminated. Moreover, the very process of "remediating" by dredging mercury-laced sediments actually had the paradoxical effect of stirring up the toxins, making them more accessible to seaborne microorganisms. In short, the solution turned out to be something of an illusion and perhaps even more of a problem than the one it supposedly solved. When the dredging was complete, engineers placed a cement and steel barrier—like the sarcophagus at Chernobyl or the clay and polyurethane cover at Love Canal—over the mercury-soaked portions of the seabed that could not be removed and buried in a toxic waste dump on land.

Even when the process was complete, no one was sure that the mercury was safely contained. Perhaps suspecting as much, the authorities have refused to conduct a full epidemiological study that would determine the full scope of health impacts from the mercury poisoning of Minamata Bay, pre- and post- "remediation." Invariably, samplings of sea sediments have revealed alarmingly high rates of mercury, as have periodic samplings of fish (which did not stop the Japanese government in 1997 from declaring fish from the bay safe for consumption). In the meantime, Japanese chemical companies, prevented by new regulations and legislation from dumping toxic wastes into Japanese rivers, seas, and oceans, often moved their operations overseas to developing countries such as Indonesia, which lacked such regulations. Japan's new environmental consciousness and regulatory apparatus, it turns out, worked only in Japan, whereas Japan's industrial giants operated throughout the world.

Back home, Minamata, like Love Canal in western New York, became a kind of pariah community, notorious as a symbol of pollution and struggling to find an identity in a postindustrial world. Like Niagara Falls, Minamata was once a thriving industrial city of more than 50,000. Today, most industry has disappeared and the population has shrunk to less than 30,000, mostly older people. Young people leave, often concealing their origins for fear of being labeled "polluted," which would make it very difficult for them to find a job or marriage partner.

Debates continued in Minamata about how, and if, to remember the disaster. Some residents wanted to forget that it had ever happened. A handful of activists—a tiny minority—argued that Minamata should be made a "sacred city," a monument to the violence of toxic waste, just as Hiroshima honored victims of the atomic bomb. A memorial erected in 1996 contained copper plates with the engraved names of the dead hidden inside a copper chest, a reflection of the continuing shame and stigma attached to victims.

The very system of compensation has also had a perverse outcome, making the victims dependent on the perpetrators. The Japanese government continually propped up the Chisso Corporation with cash infusions so that it could continue accepting its burden of shame and paying out money to survivors. Even the few Minamata residents who hadn't died or become permanently disabled and who continued fishing became dependent on Chisso. Because no one would dare eat fish from Minamata, the compensation settlement stipulated that the fishermen should deliver their catch to Chisso, which would then destroy the fish, considered officially edible since 1997, but nonetheless incinerated just in case. Fishing in Minamata had become a form of welfare, a way to support fishermen who, paradoxically, could no longer support themselves by selling their catch. Instead, they caught fish for the toxic-waste incinerator, an illustration of one of the lesser-known and more bizarre results of Japanese modernization.

SOURCES

■ **Struggling with the Disease**

The following is the story of a victim's thoughts about his quest to deal with the disease. Oiwa Keibo came from a family of Minamata fishermen—the ones most affected since they had a diet made up almost exclusively of seafood from the poisoned bay.

As you study this document, address the following questions: Why did some of the victims refuse to participate in the lawsuit against the Chisso Corporation? How did social and economic pressures divide the victims? How did neighbors look upon Keibo's family? Were they supportive, and why or why not? Why did the victims hide their suffering? Finally, what was Keibo's attitude toward being a victim, and how did that attitude clash with the necessity of playing the role of victim in order to sway public opinion?

In the 1960s, young people abandoned our region in droves to search for employment in urban centers. As televisions and refrigerators flowed in, the labor force flowed out. My family managed to keep fishing even after Father's death, but our need for cash increased. . . . It must have been when I was in primary school that instant ramen[5] appeared. Until fast foods became popular, we had been delighted just to find a fried egg in our lunch boxes.

As I grew up, I became keenly interested in politics. . . . I felt that if the government had been run properly, something as horrible as the Minamata disease incident would never have occurred. The conservative Liberal Democratic Party was in power. Therefore, emotionally I leaned toward the socialist and communist opposition parties. . . . I intuitively felt that it was not Chisso by itself but society as a whole—the system that dictated the actions of a company like Chisso—that was wrong. I understood full well that the ruling party focused its attention on the growth of such large corporations. This focus is what I wanted to change.

In 1968, the government officially recognized Minamata disease as a condition caused by industrial pollution, and the next year victims filed a class-action suit against the government. Before the suit was

---

Source: Excerpted from Oiwa Keibo, *Rowing the Eternal Sea: The Story of a Minamata Fisherman,* trans. Karen Colligan-Taylor (New York: Rowman & Littlefield, 2001), 57–60.
[5] An instant noodle soup in a container into which hot water is poured.

filed, my family was faced with the decision of whether or not to participate as plaintiffs. At that time there was only one victims' organization, but it was already divided between those who wanted to file suit and those who didn't. Those who opposed the suit worried that the costs would be so high they would jeopardize family assets, and they were concerned about alienating themselves from their neighbors. . . .

It wasn't that someone influenced me to promote the lawsuit. I reached that decision on my own. . . . I also wanted to strike back at Chisso and to clarify the company's responsibility. . . . I didn't know a thing about trials. But I did know that I had to do something to avenge my father's death. . . .

After Father died, Minamata disease became so prevalent in my family that people began to say it must be a genetic problem. In a remote village like ours, this type of gossip might well have been the product of some long-smoldering envy of a well-established family. . . . Other men in our village had died in much the same way that my father had, but no one was willing to trace the causes of their deaths to Minamata disease. If they had admitted the roots of the problem, as my family had, they in turn would have become the object of village gossip. Some rumors would hold that the disease was genetic, and some would say it was infectious. Through these rumors Minamata disease became a social stigma, which made it difficult for young people to find marriage partners or employment. If families accepted compensation for death or illness, they would be accused of taking Chisso's dirty money. So, families who lost a loved one to Minamata disease would attribute the death to any number of other afflictions. Even the victims themselves must have wanted to believe that they had anything but Minamata disease. . . .

However, as the case progressed and the issue was covered on television and in the press, Chisso's responsibility became a topic of public discussion. As the disease became more socially acceptable, the number of victims applying for certification increased. . . . My mother and brothers would often tell me that nothing we said about Minamata disease could bring my father back to life, so there was no point in discussing it. . . . I must say that among the younger victims there is a tendency to develop a dependent mentality. . . .

Diseases caused by industrial pollution are often viewed simply as tragedies for the victims. But as a Minamata disease patient, I can now say that while this disease is a tragedy, we can also look at it as an ordeal to be overcome. In this sense, Minamata disease victims are no different than other handicapped people. If we define ourselves as victims, we won't get anywhere. Only when we embrace Minamata disease as a condition with which we live will we be able to keep moving forward.

■ Those Who Remain Are Like Embers

The second document is also an excerpt from Keibo's memoir. It describes Keibo's thoughts after achieving seeming victory—the creation of a process whereby victims could be certified and qualify for compensation payments. To the astonishment of fellow Minamata activists, whose efforts he had coordinated, led, and organized for years, Keibo decided to reject the compensation. The move was all the more astounding given his single-minded commitment—including numerous arrests during acts of civil disobedience—to get justice for the victims. He had sacrificed friends and families for the sake of pushing the Minamata issue to the forefront of Japanese society.

Why do you think Keibo ultimately refused compensation? How does he invoke his religious beliefs to justify his rejection of compensation? What do you think he means when he says that compensation is a "ritual"? How does he understand the clash between tradition and modernity? What is his attitude toward the state and how can this attitude be explained? What do you think that Keibo means when he says that there "is an unbridgeable gap between the individual and the system"?

As I look back on the Minamata movement, or at current nuclear-power and dam-construction issues, I always wonder why people give in to money. Why do they settle for compensation funds or "onetime" settlement payments? What does *hosho*, compensation, mean? I have been thinking about this for a long time. I think "compensation" is a concept that entered Japan in the Meiji period, along with other concepts of modernization and Westernization. Earlier, under the oppressive authority structure of feudal Japan, one had no choice but to accept one's lot—or die. It would be a mistake, however, to think that the compensation system had been forced on the people from above. It was one of the citizen's demands in the process of democratization, and it is something we continue to demand today. We have sought out a lifestyle in which everything has a price.

Today almost all workers have been swallowed up by the Establishment, and you seldom hear anyone speak of "class struggle." You can no longer distinguish the political Right from the Left. As the economy

---

Source: Excerpted from Oiwa Keibo, *Rowing the Eternal Sea: The Story of a Minamata Fisherman*, trans. Karen Colligan-Taylor (New York: Rowman & Littlefield, 2001), 153–157.

grows, demands for compensation will increase both in number and amount. However, as capital plays a greater role in our lives, the place occupied by the soul seems to shrink. This is a situation that we, the people, have created in collaboration with the Establishment.

Of course, the reason we seek compensation is that we feel we cannot get by without it. Perhaps it has become a rite of passage, concluding an event. When a person dies, we hold a wake and a funeral, followed by seventh-day, forty-ninth day, and one-year Buddhist memorial services. Perhaps compensation is also a ritual. In this sense it does have meaning. . . .

The question still remains, however, as to why no one went one step farther, why no one kicked in the wall of the system, exclaiming, "This isn't about money!" There are some who received payment and then said, "This isn't about money." But how can you extract yourself from the system once you have been paid off?

Probably those who receive compensation, especially those who had been in the vanguard of the movement, sensed that as long as they held to the line that they were not after money, they would be exposing themselves to extreme suffering. They must have realized what would lie ahead: expulsion from society, isolation, and ultimately insanity. I understand this only too well from my own experience. Because they could foresee this fate, they chose to accept the money and withdraw their feelings into the inner recesses of their hearts. Who am I to censure their actions?

Therefore, rather than seeing the victims "taking money," I see them as withdrawing. After waiting patiently for years in the most difficult conditions and enduring all the accusations surrounding their motives, they found themselves accepting a final settlement. . . . We need to let go and return to the lives of ordinary people. If I think about those who accepted the final payment in this way, it all makes sense. . . .

There's no need for anyone to feel guilty about receiving a sum of money that would barely purchase a car. They should think of the money as "travel expenses." . . .

In the past when I used expressions like "the Chisso within us" and "the state is but another expression for ourselves," people challenged me with the question, "Does that mean, then, that you have forgiven your enemies?" Naturally, it's not easy to forgive one's enemies. For those whose very existences are determined in relation to their enemies, to lose their enemies would be to lose their own identities. That's a terrifying prospect. When I applied for certification I was not yet aware of this. I was still young. But I did not forgive the authorities. I simply threw them out of my life. I don't find the state valuable enough to want to keep on pursuing it. The state makes no attempt to assume responsibility and, in fact, is incapable of doing so. It gives you some kind of glib response, but that's not what the patients want to hear. What they want is compassion—someone to share their pain. There is an unbridgeable gap between the individual and the system. You must place your trust in one side or the other. I place my trust in the individual.

When I withdrew my application for certification, there were those who criticized me, saying, "All you are doing is satisfying the state and the company." I certainly don't see it that way. I acted to divorce myself from the state. There are still people who, as long as they live, will never say, "It's over." These people cannot be judged by the standards of the Establishment. The system is at a loss as to how to deal with them. They don't put their trust in the state but in themselves. This is also a form of resistance. . . .

Traditional peoples have been cast aside and marginalized the world over. Their numbers may be few, but their existence has become ever more meaningful. Those who remain are like embers. . . . When the system tells me, "It's all over. The fire is out," I want to be right here to declare, "No. Here are the embers. I've kept them glowing."

■ The Confrontation at Goi

The story of the Minamata victims, also reflected in the stories of many other victims of large-scale disasters, conveys a simple but profound point: Empowerment comes through struggle and sacrifice. The Chisso Corporation did not simply decide at a certain point to admit its guilt and provide compensation. It was forced to do so— and only after a long and bitter struggle. The following description is of an incident on January 7, 1972—before the Chisso Corporation finally agreed to settle a lawsuit brought by Minamata victims. The eyewitness, the American journalist W. Eugene Smith mentioned earlier, was severely beaten by Chisso Corporation employees during an attempt by Minamata patients—led by the victim activist Kawamoto—to arrange a meeting with company management in the city of Goi. As a result of the beating, Smith suffered permanent and severe damage to his vision.

Do you think the beating of the Minamata patients would have been noticed if an American journalist had not been injured? Why

Source: Excerpted from W. Eugene Smith and Aileen M. Smith, *Minamata* (New York: Holt, Rinehart, and Winston, 1975), 94–98.

was he apparently singled out for a brutal beating? Why do you think the union members at Goi sided with Chisso and participated in the violence against the Minamata victims? Do you think the company's use of violence aided or detracted from the company's attempt to avoid responsibility for Minamata disease? Why do you think the company acted the way it did? How did the protestors use Buddhist religious rituals to advance their cause against the Chisso Corporation? Why do think they did so? How did publicity surrounding the incident affect public opinion?

January 7, 1972, is a day that will long endure in my mind.

It started with Kawamoto's group traveling an hour and a half to Chisso's plant at Goi to keep an appointment. It ended with patients being mauled and me being seriously injured. My equipment was destroyed.

Chisso had ordered union members from Goi to serve strong-arm duty in front of their Tokyo offices. Kawamoto considered this wrong and made an appointment with the head of the labor union to discuss why a supposedly free union was providing manpower for this company-ordered anti-patient action.

Patients, supporters, and newsmen arrived at the gates of the Goi factory at the appointed hour. A runaround began. . . . A newsman demanding to use a telephone to meet a deadline suddenly vaulted the iron gate. The patients' supporters, triggered by this, rushed forward. . . . I photographed Kawamoto through the open gate; he was hunched slightly, as usual, talking to the guards, his hands in his pockets, and I laughed at this "riot" scene. He and his followers took a leisurely walk into the gatehouse. . . . A guard invited me to have a chair. I thanked him. . . .

I was relieved and pleased that a dangerous situation seemed to be under control. . . . yet I had been aware of the black company cars moving slowly by, surveying the scene, and of guards making frequent trips deeper into the factory for exchanges with men in work uniforms. I was uneasy.

Suddenly, a mob of workers rounded a factory building to converge on the gatehouse. I made a dash for the building, thinking of my wife, not of news. The mob pinned us in. A man started barking orders. I guessed (correctly) that he had been a sergeant in the Imperial Army. . . . They hit. They hit me hardest, among the first. After my cameras, perhaps. The last exposure, bad, blurred, shows the man on the left, his foot at that moment finishing with my groin, reaching my cameras. The man on the right was aiming for my stomach. Then four men raked me across an upturned chair and thrust me into the hands of six who lifted me and slammed my head against the concrete outside, the way you would kill a rattlesnake if you had him by the tail. . . .

Chisso had set us up—they, by damn, were going to intimidate patients and take care of that foreign journalist. . . .

They made a serious mistake. The beating of a respected American journalist loosed an avalanche of unfavorable publicity upon Chisso, and it gave increased respectability to Kawamoto and the Minamata cause: if Chisso were really like this, people said, maybe the patients were right. If I had to suffer the injury, I took consolation in the fact that it increased nationwide sympathy for the patients.

Chisso issued a written statement immediately after the incident: I had become hysterical and injured myself. . . . Chisso offered a statement of "regret," and offered to pay medical fees without admitting responsibility, if we would withdraw legal charges filed with policies. I said I wanted their lies corrected publicly. . . . They retracted nothing, they admitted nothing. The company's behavior gave me an intimate look at the frustration the patients had endured for years. I decided not to sue. I could not be both plaintiff and journalist.

In January, after the Goi incident, Chisso put up the bars that made a fortress of their office. Kawamoto . . . invented ways of rattling the gates, so to speak, such as bringing in a makeshift altar and a Buddhist priest to intone prayers for the victims, or gathering victims and supporters to bullhorn demands . . . through corridors. Occasionally there would be a brief dialogue with a Chisso manager on the other side of the bars. Once, the patients sawed for hours, cutting two or three small bars by hand. They knew, of course, it would get them nowhere. It was strictly psychological, just to say, "Remember, we are still here."

■ "Let a Feather Drop Onto Their Heads. . . . ": The Chisso Corporation Defends Itself

The Chisso Corporation dealt with the Minamata problem with a combination of carrots and sticks. Initially, in 1959, it offered "sympathy" payments to victims, token sums that did not require that the company actually admit guilt or stop its dumping into Minamata Bay.

Source: Excerpted from interview with Chisso Corporation spokesperson Keiji Higashidaira, reprinted in Akio Mishima, *Bitter Sea: The Human Cost of Minamata Disease,* trans. Richard L. Gage and Susan B. Murata (Tokyo: Kosei Publishing Co., 1992), 151–153.

At least through the 1950s and much of the 1960s, it could also count on sympathetic press coverage that constantly challenged the legitimacy and even sanity of the Minamata victims. But after the emergence of a more active civil society in Japan, public opinion began to shift, and Chisso hardened its approach. As noted in the previous document, it sometimes resorted to violence, which supplemented its strategy of stonewalling and hiring scientists to "prove" that links between its industrial wastes and Minamata disease were "inconclusive." Journalistic attitudes, however, were changing since the more conservative 1950s. The popular weekly magazine *Shukan Bunshun* on July 12, 1971, published a Japanese translation of an interview conducted by a company spokesperson with a Swedish journalist. When the company learned that the interview was to be published, it attempted, with some success, to buy up all copies of the edition of the magazine as it hit the newsstands. But not all of them were bought, and the Minamata activists reprinted the interview in leaflets that were broadly published. The incident is a powerful illustration of the key role of communications media in technological disasters. The media can support existing power structures and suppress those who challenge them, but on occasion it can also promote a change in power relationships.

How does the spokesperson attack the legitimacy of the Minamata disease activists? What is his explanation for Minamata disease? What class arguments does he advance in defense of the company? Who, according to the spokesperson, are the real victims of the court battle waged by disease sufferers for compensation? Do you think the spokesperson actually believed what he said about Minamata disease? Why do you think publication of this interview was so damaging for the Chisso Corporation?

> *Q:* Didn't you think at all of the danger of using mercury?
> *Higashidaira:* No, we never tested the mercury to find out if it was poisonous. We knew that the twenty-four other manufacturers of vinyl chlorides had been discharging untreated wastes for a long time with no obvious ill effects. Who would have thought Minamata would be the first case of pollution? We had done everything we thought necessary. It never occurred to us that our effluent was dangerous to humans.
>
> *Q:* Yet you continued pouring effluent into Minamata Bay even after 1957, when you had some idea that mercury was the cause?
> *Higashidaira:* There was no solid proof. . . .

Q: But you acknowledge now that the mercury in Chisso's effluent is the cause of Minamata disease.

Higashidaira: There may be a connection. . . . For all we know, part of the cause may be some other poisonous substance. There may be something emanating from some other place.

Q: Is there another plant nearby?

Higashidaira: No. But since we plan to go into this issue in detail in the trial now underway, I can't comment further.

Q: Do you have proof that Chisso is innocent?

Higashidaira: Of course. . . . [but] I can't, of course, give you any details right now.

Q: Are the Minamata fishers still eating fish from Minamata Bay?

Higashidaira: Yes, and that's an important point. To put it bluntly, they've been eating rotten fish that were floating in the bay. But it's difficult to make this point in court, since it would look as if we were trying to create a bad impression of our opponents. As if they were animals, you know. Those who became sick after 1958, at any rate, should be grateful that they're receiving compensation.

Q: Do you think that thirty thousand yen for each child afflicted was sufficient compensation in 1959?

Higashidaira: Yes, certainly, given the value of that amount of money at the time. The families were very glad to get the money. . . . We've done everything we can. If the victims hadn't been so poor, they probably would have gotten more money. In Japan, compensation is based on income. The Minamata fishers were barely able to earn enough to eat every day, and their prospects were quite limited. . . . In Minamata the victims were almost all old people and children.

Q: For twenty-five years Chisso spent no money on treating its wastes. You must have channeled all the money you saved into production.

Higashidaira: About fifty-fifty. The patients have cost us a considerable sum, you know.

Q: What do you think of the state of pollution in Japan?

Higashidaira: The Japanese newspapers tend to make too much of a fuss over the issue. Let a feather drop onto their heads and they'll claim it was a whole bird. As for Minamata disease, that's an issue strictly between Chisso and the patients. It's a problem of the past and has nothing to do with current issues.

Q: What do you think of the trial?

Higashidaira: Both the city and the prefecture oppose the trial. We've been forced into court. We'd prefer to solve the problem out of court, in a friendly fashion, but they won't listen. Ninety percent of Minamata residents favor mediation. It's just a few who are creating a fuss. Only a hundred fifty people turn out for their demonstrations. Most citizens want to change the city's name. Some citizens get together spontaneously and hold meetings in support of Chisso.

Q: I believe there is a growing anti-pollution movement in Minamata.

Higashidaira: They're just trying to fan the hatred. Someone's out to agitate people. It wasn't so bad at first, but now it's become a witch hunt. The patients and their families come to us making demands, and sometimes a Buddhist priest stands outside the gate intoning a sutra of mourning. It's creepy.

Q: Would you feel the same about the way the company has handled the issue if your daughter had been one of the victims?

Higashidaira: I can't even imagine that possibility.

Love Canal and the Law of Unintended Consequences

Things almost never turn out the way historical actors think they will. People anticipate one type of future—usually better than the present, according to the doctrine of progress—and they get something very different, sometimes extremely unpleasant. Love Canal is a classic illustration of the law of unintended consequences, perhaps the only law that historians agree actually operates in human history. The canal thus began as an attempt to create a new and more perfect world, a "Model City," in the words of its creator. It ended up as a toxic dump.

That astonishing and unanticipated turn of events began in the last decade of the nineteenth century and culminated in the late 1970s. In 1892, a mysterious man named William T. Love, after whom the infamous canal is named, arrived in western New York. A self-styled westerner, he promised to bring the spirit of an enterprising West back to the eastern part of the United States, in this instance to a region of New York State bordering Canada and Lake Ontario called the Niagara Frontier. Love told rapt audiences that the region had been passed over in the great rush to tame the western frontier and make it useful. Against the backdrop of the famous Niagara Falls, this P.T. Barnum-like figure spun visions of a Model City "free from defiling vapors" and from the class strife that had tainted America's burgeoning industrial centers. Fueled by "the late wonderful advance in electricity and by the aid of our limitless water power, we can heat and light our city by electricity and operate our factories by water power, in an atmosphere of ideal purity." Love published maps of a Niagara Frontier retrofitted for his vision of progress. One map depicted a 5-mile canal connecting the upper and lower Niagara River and bypassing the legendary cataract. At the canal's end on the lower Niagara, an artificial falls had been carved into the gorge, flowing into the river below and generating immense quantities of power. The envisioned power plant supported an industrial "megalopolis" to the north called Model City, which Love convinced the New York State Legislature to charter as his own personal company town. Model City, in Love's map, stretched all the way to Lake Ontario, neatly divided into boulevards and avenues. "No skill, art or effort will be spared to make it the most beautiful city in the world . . . a monument to the progressive spirit of the age—to the genius, goodness and greatness of the American people."[1]

Love's Niagara Power and Development Corporation convinced a few hardy businessmen to take up residence in Model City, and his company excavated about 3,000 feet of a canal leading northward from the upper Niagara River. Then, amidst the depression of the late 1890s, the entire enterprise collapsed. Water filled the canal. For decades, residents of the city of Niagara Falls swam and fished in the canal during the summer and skated on it in winter. By World War II, Hooker Electrochemical Corporation (later known as Hooker Chemical and Plastics Corporation) had bought the canal and transformed it into a chemical waste dump.

In 1952, Hooker threw soil on top of the waste-filled canal and essentially gave the land to the Niagara Falls School District. Desperate for land to build new schools for the postwar baby boomers, the school district was immensely grateful. It erected a school directly on

---

[1]*Description of the Plan of the Model City Located at Lewiston, Niagara County, NY, Chartered by Special Act of the New York Legislature, Designed to Be the Most Perfect City in Existence* (Lewiston, NY: The Model Town Company, 1893).

top of the chemical wastes and sold excess parcels of land surrounding the school to real estate developers. Developers built homes on those lots, a suburban utopia of white-picket fences, two-car garages, and the occasional backyard swimming pool. The newest suburb of the industrial boom town of Niagara Falls, in honor of William T. Love, carried his name, but few if any residents remembered the full history buried underneath the land they now inhabited. Focused on building a better future, they suffered from a kind of historical amnesia. How shocking, then, it was when the toxic wastes percolated to the surface in the middle 1970s, turning the American dream into a suburban nightmare and triggering a prolonged social and political crisis.

The path from utopia to dystopia—a path well traveled in all the case studies of this book—was not planned or designed. Instead, a combination of profit seeking, faith in progress, and a willingness to sacrifice the environment cleared the path to environmental crisis. Corporate titans of the electrochemical industry certainly played a primary role in the disaster, but average citizens often followed blindly down the path cleared by a host of government and corporate officials. When it came to warning about possible dangers, nearly everyone seemed to be complicit in a kind of conspiracy of silence regarding the possible risks and dangers of uncontrolled industrial and suburban development.

THE UNSPOKEN BARGAIN

It is easy to vilify Hooker Electrochemical Corporation in the Love Canal disaster, but the truth is more complex. While many tourists know Niagara Falls as one of the natural wonders of the world, industrial activity and the quest for electrical power created the twentieth-century city of Niagara Falls. Since the late nineteenth century, smoke-belching factories dominated the view on the American side of the famous Niagara Falls. Those companies used cheap hydroelectric power from the falls to produce a variety of industrial products, including chemicals, steel, and weapons-grade uranium. The Hooker Electrochemical Corporation (purchased by Occidental Petroleum after the disaster) was but one of many of the major petrochemical companies that established operations in the Buffalo–Niagara Falls region. Others included Olin-Matheson, Carborundum, Dupont, and Union Carbide (the same company responsible in 1984 for the Bhopal

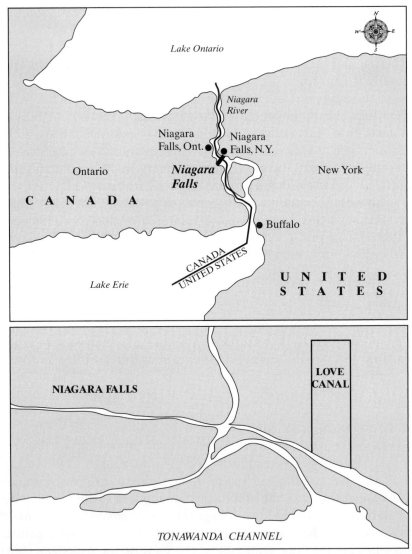

MAP 2.1   The Great Lakes region of New York, with an inset showing the Love Canal area

toxic chemical leak). The city's strategic location between Lake Erie and Lake Ontario—along the 11-mile-long Niagara River that connects the two Great Lakes and through which the entire volume of the Great Lakes water flows on its way to the ocean—made the area ideal for the production of chemicals, airplanes, guns, tanks, and cars for the war effort. A dense network of rail lines connected Niagara Falls, via

Buffalo, to points east and west as well as to Canada just across the border. Strategically situated at the geographical and industrial hub of the American smokestack economy, the Hooker Electrochemical Corporation grew from $19 million in sales in 1945 to $1.7 billion in 1978.

In the meantime, every increase in tapping the power of the falls, which fueled industrial and population growth in the city, produced a corresponding boost in toxic wastes as the by-product of these industrial activities. Hooker dealt with this problem by dumping the first chemical wastes into Love Canal in 1942, a parcel of land it bought in the 1930s before the area became filled with residents. Most accounts of the dumping, however, leave out important details. While the canal belonged to Hooker, it had become an informal dumping ground for Niagara Falls residents, other chemical companies, and the U.S. military, with whom Hooker had a contract for disposing of radioactive and chemical wastes. The U.S. Army contracted with numerous metallurgical companies in the area to produce chemical weapons and weapons-grade uranium for the Manhattan Project. As New York State investigators later learned, Hooker apparently allowed (knowingly or not is unclear) the dumping of radioactive materials into Love Canal, along with more "conventional" toxic wastes, including 13 million pounds of lindane, 4 million pounds of chlorobenzenes, and 400,000 pounds of dioxin, all highly carcinogenic. Radiological surveys in the 1980s revealed numerous radioactive "hot spots" in the Love Canal region, including a highly radioactive chunk of asphalt that ended up in a bowling alley parking lot.

Hooker may have owned Love Canal, but for all intents and purposes it was treated as a free public dump. Nearly everyone with a truck and a waste disposal problem loaded up the back of the vehicle, drove the wastes to Love Canal (usually at night), and dumped them. The more than 200 chemical agents detected in Love Canal bear witness to the incredible diversity of dumping activity at the canal. The general use of Love Canal as a common dumping ground—for the U.S. military, chemical corporations, and private citizens—suggests a much broader complicity in the creation of the disaster.

From the perspective of the twenty-first century, it may seem fantastic that people allowed such dangerous waste-disposal practices. A number of factors, however, caused people to ignore dangers. People could not fear what they did not know was a threat, and until the 1960s and 1970s, there was very little awareness of dangers associated with exposure to chemicals and almost no science investigating the problem. Until the 1970s, the U.S. government had virtually no system for regulating the storage, transport, and dumping of toxic wastes. Not until 1976 was there a federal statute to regulate the dumping of chemical wastes. The Environmental Protection Agency, cobbled together from regulating bodies in various federal agencies, emerged only in 1970, perennially underfunded and understaffed compared to other cabinet-level federal agencies. People did not think twice, as is still the case in many instances, about dumping massive quantities of pesticides, chemical fertilizers, weed killers, bug sprays, and insecticides onto their lawns, farms, living rooms, and backyards.

Finally, as the historian Hal Rothman noted, "an unspoken bargain developed between industry and workers." In exchange for "cradle-to-grave benefits," workers accepted the risks associated with living and working in a toxic environment, which at any rate were not widely understood and certainly not publicized by the few people who knew better.[2] According to an EPA survey in 1973, 60 percent of respondents had no problem living near a toxic waste dump. In short, the citizens of Niagara Falls viewed environmental degradation as the cost of progress, and progress seemed to be producing thousands of jobs in the city, so no one complained.

THE BARGAIN RE-EVALUATED

It took more than three decades for the residents of Niagara Falls to realize that environmental degradation might not be such a good bargain after all. Unlike Chernobyl or Bhopal, no single event or dramatic explosion awakened the surrounding society to a grave danger. Instead, as in Minamata, chemicals leached into the environment over decades. Similar to the frog slowly heated to the boiling point in a pot of water, citizens were hardly aware that they faced a deadly danger, until it was already too late.

Once Love Canal was full, Hooker covered the ditch with top soil and clay and sold the land to the Niagara Falls School District for the symbolic price of one dollar, a move seen at the time as an act of corporate generosity. Hooker's lawyers inserted a clause in the deed

---

[2]Hal K. Rothman, *Saving the Planet: The American Response to the Environment in the Twentieth Century* (Chicago, IL: Ivan R. Dee Publisher, 2000), 132.

that exempted the company from any health damage resulting from use of the land and it warned the school district that the soil should not be disturbed (although it was vague as to why). Seemingly oblivious to these warnings, the school district built a new school directly on top of the canal. It then sold unused land to real-estate developers, who in turn sold tracts for new housing. Following the example of Hooker, the school board inserted a clause into the deed for the tracts it sold that protected the city of Niagara Falls from being sued for health problems associated with the land. Like Hooker, the school board was off the hook.

While Hooker and the Niagara Falls school board made the disaster possible, meteorological changes triggered the events that transformed Love Canal from just another typical American suburb into the poster child of environmental disaster. The northeast part of the United States experienced an unusually wet period during the mid-1970s. Like an overflowing bathtub, the wastes in the buried canal became saturated with water and the buried toxins, including steel drums brimming with deadly carcinogens, popped through the surface. In addition, the state of New York built a new highway along the Niagara River in the late 1960s, part of the nationwide effort to promote mobility, commerce, and suburban development through car travel. Suffering from the common syndrome of historical amnesia, and thus ignorant of the location of the buried wastes, the state designed and built its road directly through one end of the canal along the Niagara River. By breaching the canal, the state inadvertently allowed the contents to leach into the surrounding area. Moreover, the road itself, once completed, blocked drainage on one side from the canal to the Niagara River. The wastes had nowhere to go but back into people's homes and backyards. Finally, as the suburb of Love Canal expanded—it was a favored destination for many aspiring middle-class workers at the chemical factories—the installation of sewer pipes provided perfect pathways for toxic wastes to migrate from the canal and into the community.

REPORTS OF MYSTERIOUS SUBSTANCES

In the mid-1970s, residents noticed a nasty black liquid percolating through the cracks of the school playground. The same jet-black substance, acrid and foul-smelling, leaked into pools in lawns and up through the sump pumps of residents living adjacent to the school. Baffled residents who attempted to gather the noxious black tar from their basements and dump it into the gutters discovered that the city intended to fine them for polluting! By the late 1970s, residents noticed that trees in backyards died and vegetable gardens would not grow. Fresh paint on houses inexplicably peeled off just months after being applied. Children rolling on the ground in the school yard suffered severe chemical burns. People burned the soles of their feet walking barefoot in their backyards. In one case, a barrel with black goo popped up beside a resident's backyard swimming pool. Neighbors swapped alarming stories of heart problems, intense nausea, multiple miscarriages, strokes, cancers, ghastly birth defects, hyperactive children, and skin rashes. The family home, the focus of the American dream and a place of supposed refuge from the dangers and insecurities of the Cold War world, had become a death trap.

As more and more journalists began reporting the strange phenomena at Love Canal, local and state officials scratched their heads and pleaded ignorance about the origins of these mysterious maladies. Fed up with bureaucratic hand-wringing, a group of Love Canal homeowners banded together on August 4, 1978, to form the Love Canal Homeowners' Association (LCHA). At its first meeting, Lois Gibbs, a shy, high-school educated mother of two young children, made the first of many public speeches. She learned about the danger of her community from articles in the local newspaper. When her son began suffering from seizures, she demanded he be transferred from the school atop the canal, but to no avail. As residents swapped more horror stories, they concluded that their lives, and those of their loved ones, were in immediate danger. The demand of the association was direct and simple: "We want out!"

The story of Love Canal activism, as with grassroots activism in the other case studies of this book, is the story of people learning hard lessons about their own system. Confronting indifference and hostility, they soon realized that their leaders did not want to hear their complaints. They learned the limits of their own power, which contrasted with the rhetoric of democracy and empowerment. Finally, Love Canal activism is the story of victims turned into perpetrators, often by their own neighbors. The last lesson was perhaps the most painful. In the god-fearing, patriotic, working-class community of Niagara Falls, speaking out against established authority was tantamount to being a "commie-pinko" agitator. During the Cold War with the Soviet Union, the term was the equivalent of being called "a Muslim terrorist" after 9/11. It was a case of blaming the messenger. Many residents denounced those who spoke out for bringing bad publicity to the city and for driving down their home values. They accused the activists of playing the role of victim to get a state hand-out. For a whole host of reasons, Love Canal activists, echoing the experience of Minamata victims, thus faced intense social pressure to keep their misery to themselves or face condemnation and rejection by their own neighbors.

If neighbor was set against neighbor, husbands often opposed their wives. Housewives dominated the LCHA. The predominance of women partly reflected a conscious decision to exploit the moral authority of women as caretakers and protectors of the children at risk. LCHA plied the media with images of deformed babies ("deformed baby of the month," Lois Gibbs once said) in order to attract attention and gain sympathy. Lois Gibbs appeared on the hugely popular daytime talk show *Phil Donahue,* watched primarily by housewives. But there were also practical reasons that women dominated Love Canal activism: Most of their husbands worked in the chemical industry. Many husbands objected to their wives' activism, fearing (quite rightly) that it might endanger their jobs. Hooker Chemical in the mid-1970s was the largest employer in the city, with 2,400 residents on its payroll. Many men feared appearing weak and helpless, especially those suffering from health ailments. Better to suffer in silence than to challenge one's masculine identity by pleading for help publicly. Lois Gibbs, for example, was stunned when she witnessed grown men crying for the first time. "The men in our neighborhood don't cry. They are he-men, the type of men who protect their families and will let nothing hurt them."[3] Tellingly, the marriage of Lois Gibbs, along with that of many other activists, ended in divorce, prompting the charge from opponents that Gibbs, far from nurturing her family, as a good housewife supposedly should, had destroyed it because of her supposed desire for notoriety, fame, and a payout.

Professional protestors and environmental activists, many of them veterans of the Vietnam War and civil rights protests who arrived from Canada just across the Niagara River, began appearing

---

[3]Lois Gibbs, *Love Canal: The Story Continues . . .* (Stony Creek, CT: New Society Publishers, 1998), 94.

in the community. Jane Fonda, known as Hanoi Jane for her expression of sympathy for Communist North Vietnam, showed up in town for a press conference and quick tour of the community, along with her radical activist husband Tom Hayden. Their presence seemed to justify the charge from opponents that the whole controversy was stirred up by outside "agitators," "hippies," and "commies."

While the community was often divided by gender, it was also split along class and racial lines. The LCHA was composed of mostly middle-class, blue-collar families. Although there were many blacks living in Love Canal, the LCHA was almost exclusively white. Those blacks, moreover, were renters and not homeowners. As the name of LCHA suggested, the organization was for homeowners and not home renters. The state system of compensation, like the LCHA, was also biased against renters. When the state and federal government finally agreed to pay to relocate about 800 families in May 1980—after a prolonged battle that included numerous arrests for civil disobedience, the taking of EPA hostages by the LCHA, U.S. House and Senate committee hearings, and the prime-time television investigative reports—renters (mostly black) received no compensation. In the meantime, homeowners just outside the "outer ring" of homes that the government agreed to buy were stuck in houses that could only depreciate in value and become the proverbial albatrosses around their necks. At one demonstration, residents burned their mortgages and tax documents, a powerful symbol of protest against the American way of homeownership.

In the meantime, local politicians and chamber of commerce members accused the resident-activists of giving the city a bad name and driving away tourists. After a national documentary called *The Killing Ground* aired in March 1979 on CBS, the head of the Niagara Falls convention center said angrily to Lois Gibbs. "I will never get anyone in there now." Gibbs snapped back: "Your convention center is worth what our houses are worth—right now, zero. Now you know how it feels to be a victim of Love Canal." When Love Canal citizens went on the *Phil Donahue Show*, Donahue remarked that the mayor of Niagara Falls reminded him of the mayor of the resort town in the movie *Jaws*: "We need to keep the beaches open. We need the tourist trade!"[4]

---

[4]Ibid., 130, 190.

The state's response was chaotic, unorganized, and improvised, which matched the fear and panic of the residents. In the midst of a brutal re-election campaign, Governor Hugh Carey of New York was furious that the disaster had complicated his campaign schedule. To most residents, he seemed to treat the disaster as a political inconvenience rather than a health emergency. His sympathies can perhaps be deduced from the job he took after retiring as governor: a highly paid consultant for the chemical and nuclear industry in the state of New York.

Finally, outsiders, and even relatives, treated the residents as if they suffered from a contagious disease, "the stigma of Love Canal," as Lois Gibbs once put it.[5] One resident remembered that her mother now refused to visit. She felt she had "the black plague."[6] Gaining a new-found sense of kinship with people across the globe in the so-called Third World, activists said their situation was similar to the "boat people" of Vietnam—refugees from the non-Communist part of Vietnam that America had abandoned during the disastrous Vietnam War. Many in the city of Niagara Falls were shocked to discover that their government seemed to care more about foreign refugees than domestic ones. "Set the Love Canal People Free," became an activist slogan, chanted in front of cameras and journalists. The slogan was a direct reference to the U.S. policy of accepting in 1980 thousands of refugees in the Mariel Boat Lift out of Communist Cuba. (A large number of them were inmates from mental health institutions and criminals dumped from Cuba's prisons by the Cuban leader Fidel Castro.) At one demonstration, a Love Canal activist held aloft a placard: "You take the Cuban boat people but not us!"[7]

SCIENCE IN THE SERVICE OF THE STATE

While Love Canal eroded the faith of many residents in their own government—local, state, and federal—scientific expertise remained a last pillar of faith for many activists. When the controversy surrounding Love Canal first gained public attention in the late 1970s,

---

[5] Ibid., 72.
[6] Sharon Kay Masters, "Life Stage Response to Environmental Crisis: The Case of the Love Canal, Niagara Falls, New York" (PhD diss., SUNY-Buffalo, 1986), 102.
[7] Image from the documentary: *In Our Own Backyard: The First Love Canal*, Bullfrog Films, 1983.

FIGURE 2.1 Tim Moriarty sits behind a facetious for sale sign attached to his front porch while holding his dog in his lap in the Love Canal area of Niagara Falls, New York. (Corbis – NY)

Love Canal victims believed state and federal scientists would work diligently and honestly to prove that Love Canal had damaged their health. If at first they assumed that science was separate from politics and economics, the unfolding Love Canal disaster, however, eventually challenged such notions.

There was a fundamental conflict of interest that lay at the heart of official, state-funded Love Canal research. If science proved that living near Love Canal was dangerous, the state would have to spend millions of dollars to move residents and clean up the problem. Money is always hard to come by, but that was especially true in the 1970s. The late 1970s was a time of prolonged economic recession, mounting government deficits, and rising unemployment. The commissioner of the New York State Department of Health once remarked: "If the choice were made to move people out before incontrovertible evidence of health damage was available, then there was a good chance of spending a great deal of money needlessly."[8] Subsequently, official studies never found incontrovertible evidence, and many activists claimed that state investigators rigged tests to generate results that justified taking no action. One test funded by the state put 22 rats in a contaminated home and had them breed. When scientists found that the first litters had no abnormalities, the state hastily arranged a press conference and declared the Love Canal area safe for human habitation. Time and again, state health officials and scientists said the data (which they usually refused to publish) were "inconclusive" regarding any link between living at Love Canal and unusually high rates of illness. Some government officials suggested that unhealthy lifestyle choices—too much smoking and drinking—had caused whatever ailments the Love Canal residents believed they had.

There were dissenting voices in the scientific community. One such scientist on the state payroll was Dr. Beverly Paigen, who worked at the Roswell Cancer Institute in Buffalo, which was funded by New York State. Paigen worked with Lois Gibbs and the LCHA to develop the "Swale Theory," which postulated that underground swales, or water conduits, provided a pathway for chemicals from the canal to leach out into the surrounding community. They then matched data regarding the location of miscarriages and other illnesses and found a correlation between people living near the swales and alarming incidences of various diseases. Paigen was shocked to discover that state officials had attacked her theory in the press before state scientists had even conducted an analysis to disprove it. The state publicly declared that the theory was "information collected by housewives that is useless," and it applied intense pressure on Paigen

---

[8]Adeline Gordon Levine, *Love Canal: Science, Politics, and People* (Lexington, MA: D. C. Heath and Company, 1982), 102.

to terminate her studies.[9] It was a common refrain that the resident-activists, mostly women with only a high-school education, heard over and over again: We (well-educated men) are the experts and you (mostly poorly educated women) are not.

Ultimately, the state acted, not because of scientific evidence but because of a combination of citizen outrage and negative media coverage. The story of Love Canal was reported on the front pages of newspapers around the world, including the Soviet Union, Japan, and India. Much of the world took pleasure in the misfortunes of the U.S. superpower, just as anti-Communists in the United States later exploited the Chernobyl disaster. Under intense pressure from local and national environmental activists, President Jimmy Carter relented and declared Love Canal a Federal Disaster area on August 7, 1978, which he followed with a second declaration of a federal emergency in May 1980, as he and Governor Hugh Carey of New York both faced uphill battles in their re-election campaign. The declarations cleared the way for a complex process by which the state of New York bought the houses of about 800 families in a so-called "inner-ring" of residences nearest the canal. The process of determining how many people to evacuate was driven less by science than by the money released for the task: about $20 million. People stuck in the outer ring were out of luck, locked into mortgages now worth far more than their houses.

Since there was no definitive science regarding health impacts, neither the state of New York nor the federal government admitted that Love Canal caused health problems. One study funded by New York State in 1980 concluded that the greatest danger to Love Canal residents was psychological, a product of the supposedly relentless media hype over the issue fueled by activists and supposedly hysterical, amateur scientists. Finally, the settlement was designed to prevent the government from actually buying the houses of the residents. Federal and state authorities wanted to avoid setting a precedent that the government would buy the homes of people who lived on or near toxic waste dumps, since it seemed likely that there were millions of people across the United States in a similar situation. Instead, the federal government offered the money as a loan to New York State, which then bought the houses as part of an "urban renewal" plan. Its plan was to resell the property at some future date to pay back the loan. The agency managing the buyout was thus dubbed the "Love Canal Revitalization

---

[9]Ibid., 93.

Authority," a convenient fiction that masked the group's true function of destroying a community rather than revitalizing it.

As with two other case studies in this book—Chernobyl and Bhopal—the Love Canal tragedy officially remains a tragedy with victims but no officially recognized perpetrators. In 1994, a judge ruled that Hooker and its parent company Occidental Chemical Corporation would not have to pay any punitive damages or admit any guilt. True, in an out-of-court settlement, it paid about $230 million to federal and state authorities, but the company had liability insurance of $320 million. The payment went toward cleaning up and maintaining the site, and not for damages inflicted on the victims or to pay for their houses and relocation. The taxpayer picked up that bill.

In the end, 800 families received money for their homes and moved out of the area. About 60 declined to move, either because they refused to believe that their lives were in danger or because they could not imagine any other place as home. Eventually, 1,300 residents received about $10,000 from Hooker Chemical for their "mental anguish" and not for any health problems related to chemicals. There has been no systematic attempt to collect data on the residents of Love Canal and to track their health (as has been the case also with most of the victims of the other disasters covered in this book). The absence of data means that the opportunity to learn about the impact of the toxic chemicals on human health has been lost forever.

LONG-TERM SOCIAL AND POLITICAL EFFECTS

The story of Love Canal is not entirely tragic. The disaster provoked a revival of grassroots democracy in the region. Many formerly excluded individuals, especially women such as Lois Gibbs, found a political voice. She moved to Washington, D.C. (the housewife who went to Washington, as she once said) and started an environmental activist group to help other communities in the United States fight toxic wastes. In the meantime, many residents of Niagara Falls discovered a simple but powerful truth: Government won't look after the interests of citizens unless citizens force it to do so. As Lois Gibbs noted, quoting Frederick Douglass: "He who wants change without struggle is like the farmer who wants crops without plowing."[10]

---

[10]Gibbs, *Love Canal*, 3.

Love Canal also focused public attention on the problem of chemical waste dumping. People in communities across the United States discovered that Love Canal was hardly exceptional. The unspoken bargain—that environmental degradation is the necessary price of progress—seemed to be breaking down, at least for a time. Federal and state authorities began creating new laws to manage the problem of toxic waste dumps. The so-called Superfund legislation provided money ($9 billion in 1986) and a system for identifying toxic wastes that made all former operators or owners of waste sites responsible for cleanup and damages. New laws also emerged that gave citizens the right—assuming they could navigate the complex rules and hire competent lawyers—to be told which chemical corporations were dumping into their environment.

Still, it remains unclear if the positive results of the disaster will endure. Lois Gibbs may have found her political voice in Love Canal, but she became persona non grata in her hometown. When Gibbs moved to Washington, D.C., to become a full-time lobbyist, the grass-roots organization she helped create back in Niagara Falls disbanded. Local activists had only mixed success in turning the single issue of Love Canal into a broader movement for environmental justice—the guarantee that the risks associated with hazardous wastes will be equitably distributed and that those who profit from producing such wastes will pay for their cleanup.

For many, faith in the possibility of effective government was another casualty of Love Canal. At first, many Love Canal activist-residents believed that their concerns could be addressed by appealing to common human decency and justice and by working patiently with government officials. But it soon became apparent that those lacking economic and political power did not matter. Government officials, many concluded, were ultimately more concerned with preserving the flow of tourists into the town and keeping chemical companies happy than with dealing with the concerns of everyday citizens. It was an especially bitter pill to swallow for the many patriotic residents of Love Canal, many of whom had sacrificed themselves in numerous wars to fight the twin threats of Nazism and Communism. Their own government, it turned out, was the enemy—and when one group of disappointing officials was elected out of office, the newly elected group seemed to be equally disappointing. For many, the disaster cut through rhetoric about democracy and revealed the vast gap dividing those with money and power and those without money and power. That lesson ultimately connects many of the people of Love Canal to many of their fellow victims in the other case studies of this book. In the next case study, for instance, powerless slum dwellers in India bore the brunt of the chemical toxins released by an American-based petrochemical company in Bhopal. As with many residents of Niagara Falls, they soon realized that they had neither the money nor the political pull to secure justice.

Meanwhile, many Niagara frontier citizens, though by no means a majority, are vaguely aware of living in the midst of severe environmental contamination. Love Canal is one of hundreds of officially recognized toxic waste dumps in the area. Long-time residents realize that informal, undocumented dumping occurred all around the region, off any map but real nonetheless. The problem is that few remember where the wastes were buried, and those who do are either dead or unwilling to speak up. Furthermore, as properties changed hands from one owner to another, the memory of toxic wastes at a site was often lost. As a result, "ownership" of the toxic waste problem also disappeared.

Exacerbating this vacuum of knowledge is a growing complacency that suggests that the "new environmentalism" from the 1970s has run its course. On one side are environmental activists, spurred on by Ralph Nader, who at a public meeting in the spring of 2005 at a school near Niagara Falls referred to the legacy of chemical and radioactive wastes in the region as an instance of "institutional insanity," "toxic terrorism," and a "silent form of violence."[11] On the other side are many neighbors of the Nader supporters. They characterize environmental activists such as Nader and Lois Gibbs as tree huggers and alarmists whose activities needlessly frighten residents, drive down property values, and scare away potential investors and tourists. The latter prefer the "unspoken bargain" referred to by historian Hal Rothman: A return to the 1950s when environmental degradation in the community and workplace was calculated as the cost of progress and maintaining jobs. That unspoken bargain lives on in western New York, as it does in all the areas covered by this book, where many believe environmental cleanup must come at the expense of economic growth. For many Niagara Falls residents—the population has shrunk from more than 85,000 in the 1970s to about

---

[11] Author's notes from Ralph Nader's speech at the Lewiston-Porter High School, Lewiston, NY, April 14, 2005.

25,000 today—protecting the environment is a zero-sum game: either jobs or a clean environment, but not both. Many would gladly trade a clean environment for a job.

In the meantime, government officials at all levels, with ever-shrinking budgets for cleanup, can see no way to rid the area of toxic wastes. They reason that since the area is already contaminated, they might as well make the best of a bad situation and develop the region's most promising line of business in the twenty-first century: the processing of chemical wastes. The area is now home to one of the largest licensed toxic waste dumps in the United States. Its manager, the Houston-based Waste Management, bragged to investors on its Web site that "we are growing," a telling commentary on the fate of William T. Love's original utopian vision for a Model City "free of defiling vapors."

"REVITALIZING" THE COMMUNITY

The Love Canal section of Niagara Falls is a surreal place and shares much in common with the "zone" around Chernobyl. In 2006, as one traveled into Love Canal, there was a vast empty space where a community once existed. The roads continued, some winding and turning into cul-de-sacs, but the houses that once lined them had disappeared. Everything was overgrown with weeds and trash: hypodermic needles, beer bottles, broken glass, plastic grocery bags, and steel drums. Sidewalks were barely visible, cracked, and sprouting various weeds and trees. In the middle of this noncommunity was a large area, 3,200 feet × 1,000 feet, raised up 30 feet and surrounded by an 8-foot chain link fence. The fenced-in area, 40 acres in all, resembled a golf fairway, only with hundreds of odd-looking pipes jutting out here and there. They are water-monitoring pipes to help determine if the 21,000 tons of toxic wastes buried in the early 1980s, along with the remains of 239 contaminated and demolished homes underneath, were leaking. The chemicals are covered with a thick layer of clay, topped by a thick polyethylene membrane that is supposed to contain any future leaks. In front of many of those pipes, the EPA has planted pine trees, a kind of "green washing" to obscure the toxic reality of this area. Rumor has it that those trees die every year and are replaced with new ones.

In the entire former community of Love Canal there is not a single sign, placard, or information booth to explain the function of the fenced-in area. It is as if a person had walked into the heart of the jungles of Belize and discovered ancient, Mayan ruins nearly completely submerged under dense jungle growth. The visitor would wonder: What happened here? Who were these people who lived here? What did they do? Why did their civilization collapse? Unlike the Maya, however, it took just two decades for people to forget about an entire community.

Erasure of the memory of the Love Canal disaster was partly inadvertent—who wants to remember unpleasant things? —but it was also a matter of state policy. In September 1988, the governor of New York declared (on what basis was never clear) that "most" of the Love Canal area could be inhabited (but not "safe"), if anyone wanted to move in. Activists who protested the resettlement received death threats. In 1996, the Love Canal Redevelopment Authority renamed the closest adjacent standing community "Black Creek Village Community Park," refurbished 234 abandoned homes, and sold them to new residents. The engine of progress sputtered and stalled as a few hardy souls moved into the far edges of the disaster zone. The deeds to the houses contained a clause that new owners could not hold the government responsible for any illnesses they might suffer in their new homes. Most of the houses, however, remained unsold, fell into disrepair, were covered with graffiti, surrounded by trash, and boarded up. When confronted with this embarrassing piece of urban blight, the city of Niagara Falls in the late 1990s finally decided that the only viable strategy for "urban renewal" was to bulldoze the homes. A local librarian argued that at least one house should be preserved as a kind of time capsule of suburban, middle-class, chemical worker life in the 1970s. She and others also argued that a museum should be created to tell the story of Love Canal, perhaps even making Love Canal into a kind of suburban apocalypse museum, a memorial to a community destroyed by progress, so that the memory of the Love Canal story would not be lost. But local boosters, politicians, and most remaining residents of the city of Niagara Falls wanted nothing to do with these plans, thereby killing all efforts to create the museum. Many agreed with the assessment of conservative pundit Michael Fumento that the Love Canal controversy was a case of "mass hysteria" lacking any scientific basis and whipped up by sensation-seeking journalists and would-be muckrakers. At most, according to Fumento, the dump was a minor nuisance that had been hyped by enterprising locals, class-action lawsuit lawyers, and ignorant journalists to bilk money out of a respectable pillar of the American corporate community. He was proud to have "exposed" the media for "lying about a perfectly safe place called Love Canal."[12]

Following the bulldozing of the "revitalized" community, city officials in 2000 built a play structure for children directly adjacent to a fence blocking access to the buried wastes. They created a nature trail that ran up to the fence called "Black Creek Park" lined with exotic plants. In another section, they built a baseball field, which, like the play structure, seemed more decorative than functional, since it was nearly always empty. A white PVC pipe stuck up out of the grass like a periscope from the underworld—another pipe for water monitoring. All of this activity took place under the direction of the Love Canal Revitalization Authority. In 2002, the state of New York finally decided it had to say something about this odd, uninhabited community. So it placed a large granite slab, about 5 feet tall and 3 feet wide, far down one side of the abandoned Love Canal region. Only a person who knew it existed could find it. The granite slab looks remarkably like a tombstone. The sole official memory of Love Canal, the granite slab lists in chronological order the various state, federal, and local agencies who responded to Love Canal. Curiously, however, the granite slab provides no explanation or even description of the emergency that caused all this government action. Nowhere is there any mention of the grassroots activists such as Lois Gibbs who forced the government to act; and nowhere is there any mention of any human suffering, health problems, or remaining challenges. The state had edited them out of the official history of Love Canal.

The public educational system has participated in this process of erasure. All high school students in the state of New York take a "Regents" exam to test their knowledge in various fields, including history. Bureaucrats construct the exam in the state capital of Albany and the performance of students on the exam is treated as a major measure of educational attainment. The section on New York history does not mention Love Canal. Since most teachers see their job as preparing their students for success, which requires that they teach to the test that measures success, it makes absolutely no sense for them to say anything about Love Canal in their lesson plans (assuming they have ever heard of it). If the intent of local and state leaders in New York is to make a complete break with the memory of Love Canal, they may be succeeding.

---

[12]"A literary Brouhaha," *Niagara Falls Reporter*, January 31–February7, 2006, 2.

SOURCES

■ A Child's Death

The following document is a statement made in 1980 by the Love Canal activist Luella Kenny to the shareholders, meeting of the Occidental Petroleum Corporation, which now owned Hooker. Along with Lois Gibbs, Luella Kenny was one of the most prominent Love Canal activists. As a result of the efforts of Kenny and others (many of them housewives of workers for chemical companies in Niagara Falls), state, local, and federal officials finally addressed the toxic waste problem at Love Canal. Their efforts were also critical in the federal government's creation of the Superfund legislation, which forced polluters to bear some of the costs for cleaning up identified toxic-waste dumps.

How do you think Occidental Petroleum executives reacted to Kenny's comments? When Kenny refers to her son's illness, does she have proof that Love Canal was responsible for it? How does she make the case of a link between Love Canal and her son's death? Does she speak with any particular authority, expertise, or special knowledge? How does Kenny link Love Canal to larger economic and political issues? What, exactly, is Kenny asking that Occidental Petroleum do?

My name is Luella Kenny. I am a cancer research assistant at Roswell Park Memorial Institute in Buffalo, New York. From July 1st 1969 to September 5, 1979 I resided at 1064 96th Street, Niagara Falls, New York, which is located approximately 0.1 of a mile from the northern boundary of the Love Canal. My husband and I with our two surviving sons were forced to abandon this residence because of the presence of toxins that had migrated from the Love Canal. Since that time we have lived a vagabond existence waiting for this problem to be resolved. An old streambed, which intersected with Love Canal, runs through our property. This streambed is now filled and is part of our yard. In addition, at the back edge of our property is Black Creek, which had been found to be contaminated with chemicals by the Environmental Protection Agency and by the New York State Health Department. Also

Source: "Statement to the Annual Meeting of Occidental Petroleum Shareholders: Corporate Responsibility Resolution May 21, 1980," in *The Palgrave Environmental Reader*, eds. Daniel G. Payne and Richard S. Newman (New York: Palgrave Macmillan, 2005), 230–231.

located on this property is a storm sewer which drains the area north of the Love Canal. Large amounts of dioxin were found where this storm sewer empties into Black Creek. My sons spent many hours playing in the creek by this storm sewer. Our seven year old son died October 4th, 1978 from complications that resulted from nephrosis.[13] This spring E.P.A. erected a six foot fence in our yard and along Black Creek because of the hazard.

Jon became ill on June 6, 1978. Nephrosis in its early stages is often masked by symptoms resembling allergies . . . Jon's death was caused by a cardiac arrest brought on by the exertion of trying to breathe . . . After Jon's death we read in the newspaper that the state of New York was going to investigate his death. It was at this time that my husband and I began to try to learn more about the disease. We began delving into medical journals, and corresponding with leading research groups in the field of nephrosis. We were shocked to find that during the past ten years there have been countless reports of people developing nephrosis when they were exposed to chemicals. We also did some research into dioxin toxicity and discovered that many of Jon's autopsy findings were related to dioxin poisoning . . . Since we left our home in September our two sons have shown a remarkable improvement . . . Dr. Beverly Paigen from Roswell Park Memorial Institute compiled an epidemiological study of the Love Canal Area. This study clearly shows the higher incidences of miscarriages, birth defects, nervous disorders and suicides just to name a few of the many illnesses that are being experienced by the residents. Many of these illnesses follow the filled in streambeds indicating a migration of chemicals. These illnesses were even more graphically portrayed when we were living in hotels last fall. It's one thing, to read the statistics, but it is something else when you have hundreds of people together under a common roof with their related illnesses.

It's amazing all of these illnesses are prefaced with the term idiopathic, that is, origin unknown. John's illness is referred to in medical journals as idiopathic nephrosis. Melissa Gibbs, the four year old daughter of the Love Canal Homeowners Association president, was rushed to the hospital last month when her blood platelet count dropped from a normal of 150,000-400,000 to 1000. She was diagnosed as having a blood disease called I.T.P. The I of course stands for idiopathic.

The following words are truer today than what they were in 1776 when Thomas Paine penned them in his American Crisis #1, he wrote

---

[13]A degenerative kidney disease.

"These are times to try men's souls." Inflation has forced both individual consumers and giant corporations to reassess their "style of living." The current political unrests that exist all over the world have left us in fear of another world war.

However, we won't have to worry about the luxuries we can't afford because of inflation, and why worry about an enemy who will destroy us when we are self-destructing. We don't need sophisticated nuclear weapons; all we need are the multitude of dumps strategically placed all over the country that will insidiously destroy everything and everyone in its path.

■ A Curious Tax Audit

Scientists and researchers who joined the activists found that they were putting their reputations and livelihoods on the line. One such scientist was Dr. Beverly Paigen, who worked for the New York Department of Health's Roswell Cancer Institute in nearby Buffalo, New York. She knew people who lived in the Love Canal region of Niagara Falls and started researching possible links between drainage canals ("swales") leading out of the former canal and unusually high incidences of various diseases among people who lived near the swales. Officials at the New York State Department of Health, including her bosses, publicly condemned the work's scientific validity without double-checking her hypothesis. As the following document illustrates, New York State's attempts to silence and intimidate Dr. Paigen may have taken other forms as well.

The document is dated July 11, 1980, a time when Love Canal residents were pushing hard to get New York State and the federal government to provide monetary compensation. Do the claims made by the state of New York seem credible? Why or why not?

Dear Dr. Paigen:
   Your letter of June 18, 1980 expressed concern that the recent audit of your 1976 tax return might in some way be connected with your activities involving the Love Canal Homeowners Association. This is a very serious

---

Source: James H. Tully Jr. (State of New York Department of Taxation and Finance) to Beverly Paigen, Ph.D., July 11, 1980, Box 4, Folder 11, 22/3F/634, Adeline Levine Love Canal Research Materials, University Archives, The State University of New York at Buffalo.

charge; and, upon receipt of your letter, I requested a full examination of the circumstances which led to the selection of your 1976 audit.

The information in our computer records and the Audit Division's files clearly indicates that your fears of bias in the selection of tax audits are unfounded. However, you are quite right in objecting to the inclusion among your tax records of clippings about your interest in Love Canal. The addition of such clippings to your audit folder was an unauthorized action resulting from a misunderstanding of Department policy by a local audit supervisor. I hope the following information about our audit selection practices and our policy regarding the use of news stories in the conduct of tax audits will convince you that normal Tax Department procedures were applied in your case, except for two unfortunate but understandable instances of human error. . . . During the course of this audit, you discovered that your tax file contained 1979 and 1980 newspaper clippings concerning your involvement with the Love Canal Homeowners Association. These had been clipped and sent to the auditor in charge of your case by an audit supervisor . . . who had misunderstood a long-standing Departmental policy. Since at least 1974, we have asked field people to clip and pass on to managerial staff local news stories involving cases of federal tax evasion and income tax delinquencies or fraud. Certainly your return did not meet these guidelines. As a result of your complaint, all field audit personnel are being reminded of the appropriate way in which news clippings may be used to supplement audit information. . . . I hope you will agree that, in all fundamental respects, the tax audit of your 1976 return followed normal, objective procedures.

Sincerely,
James H. Tully, Jr.
Commissioner

■ Passing the Buck

One of the mysteries of the Love Canal disaster was why the school board of Niagara Falls decided to build a school directly on top of some of the most toxic substances known to humankind. The following document sheds at least some light on how much the school

Source: Ralph A. Boniello (City of Niagara Falls Department of Law) to Niagara Falls Board of Education, May 5, 1953, Box 1, Folder 12, 22/3F/634, Adeline Levine Love Canal Research Materials, University Archives, The State University of New York at Buffalo.

board knew when it accepted the land from Hooker. The letter is from the City of Niagara Falls' lawyer to the Board of Education advising it about the proposed sale of land by Hooker for $1 (which subsequently the school board accepted).

If you were a lawyer trying to determine who was responsible for the Love Canal disaster, how would this letter affect your case? What does it say about Hooker's guilt? The school board's guilt? How do you think this letter might complicate the ability of Love Canal victims decades later to receive compensation in a court of law from Hooker Chemical? How might this letter influence the attitude of Niagara Falls and New York State officials toward Love Canal victims?

Gentlemen:

I am attaching herewith the original and a copy of a quit claim deed from Hooker Electrochemical Company to the Board of Education conveying to the Board a strip of land . . . This deed is delivared [sic] subject to the rights of the public in and to any and all streets and highways which cross the said premises; and further provides specifically that the Board of Education had been advised by the Hooker Electrochemical Company that the above premises have been filled, in whole or in part, . . . with waste products resulting from the manufacturing of chemicals by the Hooker Company, and that the Board assumes all risk and liability incident to the use thereof.

It also provides that as part of, and consideration for, the said conveyance, and as a special condition thereof, no claim, suit, action or demand of any nature whatsoever shall ever be made against the Hooker Electrochemical Company, its successors or assigns, for injury to any person or property in connection with, or by reason of, the presence of industrial wastes. . . . In the event that the Board shall accept this deed, it is my opinion that there is placed upon the Board the risk and possible liability to persons and/or property injured or damaged as a result thereof arising out of the presence and existence of the waste products and chemicals upon the said lands . . . In the event that the Board accepts this conveyance, there is a possible liability on behalf of the Board of Education arising out of continued use of these premises for the deposit of waste products . . .

Very truly yours,
Ralph A. Boniello
Deputy Corporation Counsel

■ And Who Was Responsible?

The following document is the sworn statement of Frank Ventry, taken in July 1978 as part of New York State's investigation into Love Canal. Ventry was a Niagara Falls employee responsible for managing part of the Love Canal dump. The document concerns a little known aspect of Love Canal: its exploitation as a dumping ground for radioactive materials used, among other things, for the bombs dropped on Hiroshima and Nagasaki. The state of New York conducted the investigation for two reasons. First, it wanted to implicate the federal government in the Love Canal dump in order to force the federal government to help pay for the cleanup. Second, it wanted to find out why certain parts of the Love Canal dump tested positive for radioactive substances.

Based on Ventry's testimony, are you convinced that the Army should have been held liable for contamination at Love Canal? Why do you suppose that it never was held liable—and that Hooker Chemical (now Occidental Petroleum) typically gets all the blame for the dump, even though most everyone seems to have used the Love Canal as a dump? What does the testimony reveal about waste management practices in the late 1940s and early 1950s? What does the testimony reveal about the role of the press in Love Canal? Why do you suppose that the investigators could not find evidence, other than oral testimony, for the Army's dumping activities? What does Ventry's testimony suggest about the relationship between secrecy, national security, and environmental contamination? Finally, do you believe him when he says, "I have nothing to gain or lose on this?"

I am a past employee of the City of Niagara Falls. Term of employment—$38\frac{1}{2}$; years. I have nothing to gain or lose on this. Approximately two months ago I had occasion to go to the Niagara City Hall where I spoke with the City Manager, Mr. Dan O'Hara. At that time Mr. O'Hara asked me if I knew anything about Love Canal. I said yes, I filled the canal. Then Mr. O'Hara asked me what happened over there that is causing this problem. I told him that most of the factories in the surrounding area dumped including the Army. Quite some time after that occurred,

---

Source: Sworn testimony of Frank Ventry, retired city worker of Niagara Falls, July 19, 1978. (Albany, NY: New York State Archives).

a reporter came and talked with me and the results of those conversations were placed in the newspaper and I have received numerous calls from concerned citizens and others since that time. The City took over the dump from Hooker some time around 1949 and 1950 and that is the time that I started working at that site. Prior to that time, I understood that a contractor, Bud Wagner, was employed by Hooker to grade the south side of the canal. Also, Walter Credensky had machines for grading and backfilling the south side of the canal. With reference to the Army incident, I recall three specific times that the Army disposed of material in the Love Canal area. Each time a Captain arrived in a jeep with his driver and a six by six truck, Army color, perhaps with stripes on the bumper, perhaps with number 17, which comes to mind. Each time prior to unloading the truck, I was requested to loosen up the dirt in the area where the drums were to be dropped from the truck to provide a cushion effect. Then the drums were pushed into the water with a bulldozer by myself. The drums were a little smaller than 55 gallon drums, however the shape was different, more like a beer keg. The markings on the drums were yellow stripes and the exterior of the drums appeared as if they were covered with lead or zinc. The outer coating was painted with Army olive drab color. There were five men and one officer in each party, three men normally handled each drum and the men wore rubber gloves and fatigue clothing. Drums were skidded off the back of the truck. The officer in charge, the Captain, wore a side-arm. To the best of my memory, the men stated that they came from the plant on Buffalo Avenue. At this time the Director of the Public Works indicated that the Army plant was closing down and being taken over by one of the civilian plants. Army personnel did not request me to sign any documents or receipt for material placed in the dumps. At no time during my tenure of responsibility in the Love Canal area was I required to sign for material placed in the dump nor maintain an inventory of material dumped therein. There was no specific criteria [sic] to reject material from being dumped. Anything delivered was placed in the dump, about 30 or 50 truckloads a day. . . . Unrelated to Army dumping, I stated that on one occasion I had purchased a new pair of workboots and during that day they became wetted with chemicals from the dump. That evening prior to entering my home I removed the boots and left them sitting in the garage overnight. The next morning in preparation to return to work I found only the soles and heels of the boots remaining. The uppers were entirely eaten away. I also related that many times chemically-filled drums would explode or ignite when the contents of the drums contacted the water in the canal. The above statement is true and correct to the best of my knowledge.

3

The Bhopal Gas Tragedy:
A Perfect Storm of Injustice

Just before midnight on December 2, 1984, hundreds of gallons of water accidentally poured through rusted and corroded pipes at the Union Carbide pesticide plant in Bhopal, India. Inexplicably, those pipes were connected to a tank that contained chemicals used in the production of the pesticide Sevin. Contrary to proper procedures at the plant, which required that the water and chemicals not mix, the water rushed into the tank containing the chemical compounds and triggered a runaway reaction. Nearly 50 tons of the lethal chemical methyl isocyanate (MIC) formed a massive toxic cloud and burst out of the storage tank and into the surrounding air. Like a proverbial biblical plague, the deadly fog descended upon Bhopal residents as they slept in the early hours of a Monday morning, an unusually cold and still winter night for central India. Since the toxic miasma was three to four times heavier than air, it hovered menacingly over the top 20 feet of the ground, a wall of death pushing into the surrounding slums and through the open windows and doorways of the shanties. In the course of a few hours, at least 2,000 residents suffocated to death. Thousands more would die in the days that followed.

The complete lack of preparation for such a disaster amplified the tragedy and fueled the firestorm of political controversy that has raged, on and off, ever since. The chief of police in Bhopal and the top medical officer pleaded with Union Carbide officials locally and in the U.S. headquarters to reveal the nature of the leak and any possible antidote to the gas, but nobody seemed to know. Even as victims lay dying in the streets of Bhopal, Union Carbide officials insisted the gas was a minor irritant and not life threatening, though in actuality the gas destroyed the mucous lining of the lungs and other sensitive parts of the body, suffocating and blinding victims. "It is something that really can not go away from my memory, something that is so grotesque, so gory and so miserable that you really can't get over it," recounted the police chief many years later.[1] The police chief was one of the lucky victims. He survived with about 80 percent of his lung capacity permanently destroyed.

The deadly fog followed a class-based path of destruction. As the fog moved over the lake separating the slums of old Bhopal from the middle- and upper-class Bhopal on the hills, it dissipated, sparing the privileged and elite sectors of Bhopal (mostly Hindu) from the horrors suffered by the city's impoverished (mostly Muslim) masses. It was a seemingly perfect storm of injustice, combining natural forces, the industrial revolution, religious divisions, and class inequities. All the ingredients for political controversy were in place: stark evidence of the inequitable burdens of pollution borne by the poor and powerless, the seeming victimization of a former European colony by a U.S.-based multinational, and the concentration of suffering among poor Indian Muslims rather than the privileged Hindus. Aggravating the situation was the assassination of India's prime minister Indira Gandhi less than three months earlier, an act that had created a national political atmosphere of paranoia, hysteria, and suspicion.

In the following days, doctors treated nearly 200,000 people—nearly a quarter of Bhopal's population—for severe burns, blindness, and a witch's brew of respiratory ailments. Cattle, dogs, rats, and humans lay dead in the illegal shantytowns that had sprung up around the factory. The leaves of trees turned black, and eyewitnesses recalled the pungent smell of burnt chili peppers in the air, the result

---

[1]Interview conducted in Bhopal by the author with Swaraj Puri, July 9, 2008.

of a futile attempt by residents to counteract the deadly effects of the gas. Perhaps 10,000 died in the first week, but no one knows for sure since hundreds of unidentified bodies, many beggars with no identification, were cremated before an accurate count could be made (some say deliberately, in order to minimize the human toll). Victims reported hearing local government health officials declaring through loudspeakers five days after the tragedy: "Identify your dead within one hour or else the bodies will be burnt without identification."

For a variety of reasons, the plant was an industrial accident waiting to happen. Investor pressures to reduce costs and increase profits had created an atmosphere in which safety was sacrificed. A general climate of complacency, including the shutdown of nearly all safety systems during the night of the accident, was compounded by poorly trained and inattentive workers who failed to notice the sudden influx of water into the chemical tank. A plant model that would even allow the possibility of water entering the tank suggests a fundamental design flaw. Finally, the Indian government, which was part owner of the plant, overlooked safety procedures precisely because they were so eager to increase the production of pesticides for India's agricultural sector, which had suffered from chronic and paralyzing famine. Indeed, the sense of urgency that led to cutting corners at the Bhopal plant ultimately came from the circumstances that shaped India's program of modernization in the 1960s. The Bhopal accident, it turns out, was the bill come due for a carelessly executed government strategy to lift India out of poverty, overcome the scourge of famine, and fulfill the original promise of India's postcolonial independence. The story briefly turns to that historical background before returning to an examination of the disaster's cause and aftermath.

INDIA, UNION CARBIDE, AND THE GREEN REVOLUTION

India's independence from the British Empire in 1947 coincided with the beginning of a global competition between the capitalist United States and the socialist Soviet Union. Both offered two radically different approaches to modernization, one based on free enterprise and the other on complete state control of the economy. By the 1950s, especially after the Chinese communist revolution in 1949 and the popularity of Soviet-inspired freedom movements in Asia and Africa,

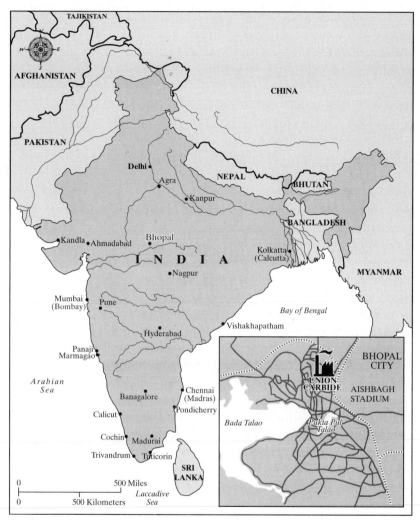

MAP 3.1   India, with an inset showing Bhopal

India allied itself much more closely with the Soviet model of state control and economic planning than with the American capitalist system. India's first prime minister, Jawaharlal Nehru (1947–1964), was deeply impressed by the Soviet socialist model and its ability to create modern industries and urban centers without the aid of capitalism. He therefore borrowed the concept of state-directed industry from the Soviet Union as well as its orientation toward rapid modernization based on heavy industry. Nehru also had an abiding faith in the ability of science and technology to lift India from its status as a former colony into a fully developed nation capable of expressing and defending its interests on the world stage, much as the Bolshevik Revolution seemed to have transformed Russia.

Economic crisis, especially in the agricultural sector, nonetheless caused a shift in Indian economic development policies after Nehru's death in 1964. During the mid-1960s, under the rule of Nehru's daughter and successor Indira Gandhi, India suffered a series of disastrous droughts, followed by mass famine. Soviet guidance and food aid was of little help, given the disastrous state of Soviet agricultural policies and practices. Nehru's development strategy, in short, seemed to have failed, although few Indian politicians dared to admit this openly. Prime Minister Gandhi responded, reluctantly and tentatively, since she remained closely allied with the Soviet Union and ideologically opposed to unbridled capitalism, by opening the nation's economy to capitalist multinational corporations. At the same time, to preserve the politically important line of hostility toward capitalism and former colonizers, Indian bureaucrats maintained tight control over foreign multinationals and required that local operations and management be staffed exclusively by Indian nationals. The byzantine system of bureaucratic control and red tape was known as "license Raj" (which was fully dismantled only in the 1990s), and it implied an economy that combined government industry and control of the economy with the limited participation of capitalist multinational corporations. The result of these policies was that India opened up its economy to American corporations in the late 1960s, especially U.S. petrochemical companies; they produced chemical fertilizers and pesticides, which promised to alleviate India's seemingly interminable agricultural crisis.

The gradual shift in policy allowed Union Carbide, a Connecticut-based chemical giant, to gain a toehold in the Indian chemical industry in the late 1960s. With the personal approval of Prime Minister Gandhi, Union Carbide chose Bhopal for a new pesticide plant because of its location at the hub of India's rail lines in the Indian heartland, the capital city of the state of Madhya Pradesh, home to a growing state bureaucracy but without a solid industrial base to promote further growth. It assembled a team of Indian nationals to provide management and also to operate the plant. Union Carbide owned 51 percent of the company—a controlling interest—and Indian authorities and private investors retained the remainder of shares, thus making the Indian government a partner in the production of pesticides.

If the appearance of Union Carbide in the Indian market reflected a shift in Indian development strategy, it was also part of the broader "Green Revolution." When Union Carbide opened its pesticide plant in Bhopal in 1969, government officials in the United States and India hailed the move as part of a Green Revolution to end famine and perpetual crisis in the agricultural sector of the third world. A broad coalition of Western interests—governmental bodies as well as Western industrial and agricultural corporations—had earlier promoted the Green Revolution in Latin America and Asia. Green Revolution advocates promised a horn of plenty for the third world. While they were genuinely keen on ending famine and starvation, many Green Revolution advocates were also driven by a desire to score political points against the Soviet Union and to promote the interests of American agribusiness. An exercise in massive technology transfer, the Green Revolution essentially meant the application of the petrochemical industrial revolution to the age-old agricultural enterprise in India, just as scientists, chemical corporations, and a new breed of farmers had done in the American Midwest. Agronomists and other experts thus consulted on new types of crops and chemical fertilizers. American corporations sold high-yielding varieties of wheat and rice to the third world. Consultants, partly sponsored by the Rockefeller Foundation, other philanthropic organizations, and U.S. development officials drew up plans for new irrigation systems. Finally, well-connected multinational petrochemical companies, such as Union Carbide, set up subsidiaries in the developing world to produce the chemical fertilizers and pesticides that would make progress bloom and starvation, like so many aphids, beetles, and earwigs, die on the vine. The effort, it should be noted, did help improve agricultural yields, prevent mass starvation, and transform India into an exporter of grain by the late 1970s (one scholar estimates that two billion people throughout the world were able to eat thanks to the Green Revolution).

Indeed, at least before the accident, Union Carbide offered a seemingly irresistible win-win scenario to Indian politicians: The company provided technology and expertise, and the country's elites got credit for modernizing agriculture, creating modern factories for India's cities, and providing industrial jobs for locals. The local press, taking a cue from official support for the company in New Delhi, feted the company as an agent of Indian progress. Bhopal politicians and Union Carbide officials rubbed elbows at the company's sumptuous guesthouse on a hill across the lake from the new factory on the outskirts of old Bhopal. When champagne flutes chinked and the topic of Union Carbide came up in political circles or in the media—at least before the disaster—no one talked about environmental issues. They discussed jobs and progress, not safety and emergency response systems. They looked at the future through a lens that filtered out any possible negative outcomes. No wonder, then, that the local authorities in Bhopal on the night of December 2, 1984, were completely unprepared for the accident. They were unable to imagine that it was even possible.

COMPLACENCY

The years between the opening of the plant in 1969 and the disaster of 1984 were ones of growing complacency about potential safety problems. The most striking aspect of local press coverage of Union Carbide in that period was the almost total absence of criticism and skepticism. Lulled into a false sense of security, corporate and government officials dismissed occasional warning signs of safety problems.

The documentary evidence for carelessness on the part of both Union Carbide employees and Indian government officials is overwhelming. Neither the company nor local police and government bureaucrats had any emergency evacuation plan for a chemical leak. Through the late 1970s and by the early 1980s, loyal officials were favored over the troublemakers who complained about safety. In order to fulfill Indian state requirements for native Indian staffing and management of the plant, many poorly trained individuals were allowed to work at the factory. The company continually downgraded the status of operators on the assumption that running operations was as easy as stoking a coal furnace, an assumption, incidentally, also shared by Soviet officials with regard to operators at Chernobyl. The more the operation of the plant appeared routine, the more the company viewed the job of operator as routine, low skilled, and therefore low paying. In the meantime, the Bhopal plant regularly exposed workers to toxic chemicals. They did not have the equipment recommended in the safety manuals, which were available only in English, even though many of the workers at the plant could not read English.

In line with a broader cost-cutting campaign at Union Carbide internationally in the early 1980s—a time of prolonged recession in the West and of extreme pressure from Wall Street for corporations to cut costs—the company laid off workers and encouraged early retirement, demoralizing employees and creating an atmosphere of carelessness. The company slashed operating and maintenance shifts in the months leading up to the disaster. Union Carbide headquarters last sent an inspector to the Bhopal plant two years before the disaster, and he had reported numerous violations, including signatures on safety reports written in English from maintenance people who could not read English. On the night of the disaster, there was not a single trained engineer on staff, and most safety systems were shut off (as in the next case study about Chernobyl). As early as 1976, two trade unions had complained about chemical leaks at the plant, and the union complained again about leaks in 1983 and 1984—not coincidentally, in the midst of a corporate cost-cutting campaign initiated at the Danbury, Connecticut, headquarters. In this climate, operators clearly understood that attention to safety issues could stall promotion. And so the list goes on. A more general concern with cutting costs, initiated in the United States, thus created a climate in which subsidiaries felt pressured to sacrifice safety.

Indian officials, who were part owners of the factory and thus benefited from its operations, were also complicit. While there were many safety rules and regulations, there were few inspectors or overseeing politicians with the will or desire to enforce them. Just as Union Carbide officials in the United States seem to have assumed that local Indian managers and government officials would adequately handle safety concerns, Indian officials seem to have believed that Union Carbide could be trusted to manage any problems that might arise at the plant. The result was that when it came to the safety of the plant and surrounding population, no one took charge. Perhaps the greatest indication of Indian government complicity emerges from an examination of the history of the area where the plant was located. When Union Carbide opened its factory in 1969, it was located, as Indian industrial regulations required, at least six kilometers away from human settlement—at that time, on the far outskirts of Bhopal. In the intervening years, however, the population of Bhopal grew rapidly, especially the population of squatters and poor people in the older and less-developed sections of the city. By the late 1970s, when the plant began producing the lethal MIC (although

Union Carbide believed the chemical was relatively harmless until the Bhopal disaster), illegal slums and shantytowns had pushed up against the walls and gates of the factory. Focused on building the future, a kind of historical amnesia afflicted local and state officials, who forgot that nobody was supposed to inhabit the areas surrounding the factory.

Even if the government had wanted to move squatters away from the factory, which it did not, evicting people from the slums would have been politically impossible. Dr. N. P. Misra, who coordinated medical relief efforts in Bhopal and who testified on behalf of the Indian government against Union Carbide in American courts, noted: "[Squatters] were all living in shanties without anyone's permission. And the government couldn't evict them . . . If the government touche[d] them, there [would be] demonstrations by political parties opposed to the government." Those who say the government should have prevented encroachment by squatters therefore need to understand, "that this is in retrospect. This is a post-mortem."[2]

Perhaps hindsight is twenty–twenty, as Dr. Misra suggested, but one thing is clear: The accident disproportionately afflicted the poorest people of Bhopal. Toxic waste disasters are not indiscriminate killers. In the shantytowns of Bhopal, as in Love Canal or Minamata, those who were poorest and least powerful suffered the most, a most unwelcome and unanticipated consequence of industrialization in India. The disaster brought these injustices into sharp relief, providing an explosive and heated framework for subsequent discussions about legal liability, compensation, and the role of multinational corporations in India's future.

CORPORATE AND POPULAR RESPONSES

If the deadly gas dissipated within days of the leak in December 1984, legal and political controversies sparked by the disaster continued to smolder. Union Carbide officials were shocked and horrified by the tragedy; they hardly fit the caricature of callous and greedy murderers created by many Indian politicians and journalists. To show its concern, the company offered $7 million in immediate aid and sent its

---

[2]Interview conducted by the author in Bhopal with Dr. N. P. Misra, July 10, 2008.

CEO, Warren Anderson, to India. He was arrested when he arrived but was soon released and allowed to go back to the United States, where he has remained in hiding ever since. Other company actions, however, revealed very different concerns. Preventing a collapse in share price, rather than admitting any guilt or attending to the victims, was a central theme of the company's press releases—understandable in business terms but certainly not likely to earn the company sympathy in the eyes of public opinion. The company, moreover, presented itself to its shareholders as a victim of unscrupulous politicians, attorneys, and incompetent reporters. Union Carbide, said its chief public relations officer, was "recast . . . as an archetypal multinational villain, exploiting India's people and resources . . . it became evident to us that this caricature was designed to gain access to Union Carbide's financial resources."[3]

The company's explanation of the accident also provoked controversy. The explanation emerged one year later from the accounting firm Arthur D. Little, which Union Carbide had commissioned to present its version of the events. According to the official company narrative, which the company maintains to this day, a disgruntled employee (in some versions, an antigovernment Sikh terrorist) had sabotaged a batch of the chemical MIC by adding water to the storage tank, thus causing the chemical explosion reaction. The Indian government, Union Carbide claimed, in turn "sabotaged" this sabotage theory by intimidating witnesses and suppressing evidence. As with most conspiracy theories, the absence of proof was the proof. The believability of this version, it should be noted, may have been enhanced by the assassination of Prime Minister Indira Gandhi by her Sikh bodyguard in October 1984—just months before the Bhopal accident.

Curiously, Union Carbide's sabotage theory paralleled popular conspiracy theories among residents of Bhopal and various activist groups. The Indian government occasionally encouraged such theories, perhaps as a way to divert attention from its own role in the disaster. Union Carbide, in popular explanations, assumed the role of victimizer and even war criminal. According to one theory, spread by the rumor

---

[3]Jackson B. Browning, Retired Vice President, Health, Safety, and Environmental Programs, Union Carbide Corporation, "Union Carbide: Disaster at Bhopal," 1993, http://www.bhopal.com/pdfs/browning.pdf (accessed June 5, 2009).

mill and sensationalistic local press reports, Union Carbide supposedly had been developing new chemical agents for the Pentagon at a super-secret facility near the Bhopal plant. "Carbide Was Carrying Out 'Shady' Research," screamed one typical headline in the local newspapers immediately following the accident. The chemical release, according to some journalists, was thus part of an experiment to test new chemical weapons on Bhopal residents. As if to strengthen the claim of Union Carbide's criminal and terroristic intent, local newspaper headlines and activists routinely referred to the gas leak as a "holocaust" and a "genocide." "The dead in Bhopal, like Hiroshima and Nagasaki, have paid the price of Union Carbide's folly in building a plant right inside a town which is a thickly populated area," said one typical article in a Bhopal newspaper.[4] A memorial to the victims strengthened the comparison to the atom bomb—and to the Nazi death camps. In 1986, a Dutch environmental activist and amateur artist donated a concrete statue of a woman and a baby to the citizens of Bhopal. Local officials erected the statue outside the gates of the Union Carbide facility. The inscription reads: "No Hiroshima, No Bhopal, We Want to Live." On every anniversary of the tragedy, activists outside the statue burned the figure of Warren Anderson in effigy, as they continue to do to this day. The Dutch artist was herself a survivor of the holocaust whose parents had perished in Nazi death camps. Her artistic commemoration of the tragedy thus connected the U.S. bombing of Hiroshima, the Nazi death camps, and the Bhopal gas leak as equal acts of premeditated murder. The implication was clear: Since the gas tragedy supposedly resembled the Nazi gas chambers, Warren Anderson was Bhopal's Hitler.

Hardly anyone, from corporate and government officials to victims and leftist activists, seemed able to accept mounting evidence that Bhopal was an unintended consequence, a tragic accident rather than a terrorist plot. Union Carbide wanted to finger the supposed saboteur for the blame; activists and many Indian politicians preferred a story about Union Carbide's deadly, genocidal experiments—an explanation that reinforced decades of political rhetoric about the evils of former colonizers and predatory capitalists and that echoed the conspiratorial mindset of Indian politics in those dark years. Similarly, many of the vocal activists could never acknowledge the inappropri-ateness of their favorite metaphors of "holocaust" and "genocide," which implied a criminal intent akin to the Nazi final solution for

---

[4]"Bhopal Tragedy Similar to Hiroshima," *Free Press*, December 1, 1985, 3.

Jews. "If ever there was a wretchedly undignified hideously helpless form of megadeath after Hiroshima and Nagasaki, this is it," proclaimed one Indian journalist.[5] Perhaps those metaphors satisfied the intense anger and grief of survivors and victims—in the summer of 2008, many victims expressed their view that the bombing of the Twin

FIGURE 3.1 Corpses lie on the ground after a leakage of poisonous gas from a Union Carbide pesticide factory in Bhopal, India, 1984. (AP Wide World Photos)

---

[5]"Diary from Bhopal," *Times of India*, December 6, 1984, 1.

Towers was just revenge for the crimes of American multinationals—but they were historically inaccurate. Unlike the bombing of Hiroshima or the gassing of Jews in Auschwitz, the Bhopal disaster was an accident. Its chief cause was carelessness—not only on the part of Union Carbide but also on the part of Indian bureaucrats, Indian operators at the plant, and Indian politicians who had ignored their own regulations about preventing settlement near the factory.

FINGER POINTING

In the supercharged atmosphere after the accident, Union Carbide developed a new explanation of the tragedy to supplement its sabotage theory: mismanagement by the company's local Indian Staff. Company officials in the United States claimed that they were hamstrung by Indian red tape, regulations, and corrupt officials. Such a disaster, they argued, could never happen in a Union Carbide plant in a more developed, fully capitalist country. Conditions were so bad that the company insisted (despite its majority ownership of the Indian subsidiary) that "majority ownership did not imply control."

Unfortunately for Union Carbide, subsequent events made many doubt that Bhopal was exclusively a "third world" phenomenon or product of excessive Indian state interference in corporate management. Residents of Institute, West Virginia, were horrified to learn that the Bhopal plant was their sister plant. Following the Bhopal disaster, enterprising reporters in the United States began to discover a story of carelessness eerily reminiscent of Union Carbide's Indian operations: frequent leaks, the absence of emergency response systems, technical breakdowns, and damning safety inspection reports. For West Virginians, the disaster was as much a reminder of the forces that united the first and third worlds as it was proof of their fundamental difference. Said one 18-year-old in Institute after Bhopal, "This incident in India kind of brings it home, doesn't it?"[6] Then, in August 1985, Bhopal's renovated sister plant in West Virginia sprang a leak (reported back in India with more than a hint of sarcasm and schadenfreude). As it turns out, the company had just touted new safety systems and processes at the plant

---

[6]"Jobs and Risks are Linked At Sister Plant in the U.S.," *New York Times*, December 5, 1984, A1.

that guaranteed, it claimed, that Bhopal could never happen in America. One hundred people within the plant were treated and 28 hospitalized. An EPA official admitted that the supposedly safer chemical compounds at the West Virginia plant were just as deadly as the ones that killed so many at Bhopal, although he couldn't say for sure, since nobody in the U.S. government had ever studied the issue. "Union Carbide probably has the best information," he told a reporter.[7] With the leak in West Virginia, many Americans suddenly realized they shared much more of a connection with India than they had ever imagined. National and local cultures certainly shaped technological practices, but just about everyone, in the interest of creating jobs and progress, seemed willing to write safety off as an unnecessary cost.

THE LEGAL DRAMA

The more people investigated the Bhopal disaster, the more the tragedy appeared to transcend conventional national borders and boundaries. How does an individual get justice from a complex multinational and multigovernment operation? To whom did Union Carbide, ostensibly a U.S.-based company, answer, when its own subsidiary in India carried its name but was extensively regulated by Indian bureaucrats and managed by Indian nationals? No one knew the answer. At first, victims attempted to sue Union Carbide in the United States, since it was a U.S. corporation, and U.S. courts tended to give out far larger awards in cases of corporate malfeasance. Victims received inspiration from dozens of entrepreneurial U.S. tort lawyers who hopped on airplanes to Bhopal almost immediately in search of victims to sign up for court cases, a phenomenon dubbed at the time as "the great ambulance chase." One Indian newspaper, three weeks after the accident, reported that "hordes of American lawyers have descended on this ravaged town like a flock of vultures . . . out to make money out of the misery of the people." One of those ambulance chasers responded in the newspaper *Indian Express*: "I'd rather be an ambulance chaser than a coffin maker. Those other people caused the accident. We're trying to get some compensation."[8] At any rate, within

---

[7]"Carbide Blames a Faulty Design for Toxic Leak," *New York Times*, August 13, 1985, A1.
[8]"U.S. Lawyers Cash in on Calamity," *Indian Express*, December 27, 1984, 7.

months, 145 suits against Union Carbide were filed in U.S. state and federal courts demanding $100 billion in compensation. Those suits involved nearly 30 law firms representing 148,000 victims (many would-be victims signed up with multiple law firms).

As the legal drama unfolded, the Indian government argued that the Bhopal case must be held in U.S. courts. It claimed the Indian court systems were filled with backlogs of cases, and Indian courts lacked the competence to handle such a complex case. In effect, the Indian government claimed its own court system was incompetent.[9] Of course, the Indian officials were well aware that the Union Carbide subsidiary in India (partly owned by the Indian government) had only about $80 million in assets, while the parent in the United States had assets of $10 billion available to pay damages. It makes sense to go fishing where the big fish are.

Union Carbide, for its part, argued that Indian courts were perfectly capable of handling the case—and to argue otherwise, it added, was to denigrate the competence of the Indian government and thus to perpetuate old attitudes of colonial dependence. Union Carbide seemed untroubled that its legal position directly challenged its other key claim that the accident resulted from the incompetence of its local subsidiary and of Indian managers, inspectors, and government officials who prevented proper plant operation. When it came to explaining the accident, Union Carbide pointed the finger at Indian incompetence, government interference, and corruption; when it came to trying the case, Union Carbide claimed Indian courts were models of legal efficiency and competence.

After much legal wrangling, American courts, within a year, finally decided that India was the appropriate venue for the case. The decision was a direct rebuke to the Indian government, which had claimed that a parent corporation should always be responsible for the actions of its subsidiary—a questionable proposition in the murky area of international law governing multinational corporations. As one scholar noted, technology easily transferred from the United States to India; but legal liability for that technology did not transfer back from India to the United States.

The other murky legal issue concerned who should have the right to represent victims. American tort lawyers argued that they

---

[9]"India Wants U.S. Courts to Handle Bhopal Cases," *New York Times*, December 7, 1985, A33.

should have the right to represent the victims in American courts. (Such lawyers typically received a third of the damage awards as their fee.) To maintain control over the process—and to prevent American lawyers from profiting and victims from transforming the case into a political movement—the Indian parliament passed an act that designated the Indian government as the sole legal representative of the victims. Many American lawyers, eager to represent Bhopal victims, argued sensibly, if selfishly, that the Indian government had a conflict of interest in representing the victims, since Indian governmental policies may have contributed to the disaster.

While the Bhopal case dragged on, the Indian government fired the minister of labor for the state of Madhya Pradesh and the state's chief inspector for factories. A handful of Indian Union Carbide managers were arrested. But within three years of the accident little else happened, as the Indian government continued to hold out for as much money as possible from Union Carbide—an out-of-court settlement it hoped would placate political interests at home, prevent the case from ever going to trial, and stop a closer inquiry that might reveal its own complicity in the disaster.

In the meantime, increasing numbers of Bhopal residents had registered as victims, in many cases by paying bribes to judges and local officials. By the end of 1988, 550,000 people had applied for relief as victims—more than half the city's population. The first Indian judge who presided over the case, and then later another judge, had to resign when it turned out that they, too, had signed up as victims. Eventually, 1.2 million people sought compensation as victims of Bhopal—more than the entire population of the city! People filed claims from as far away as Moscow and London, claiming they had been gassed when they passed near Bhopal shortly after the leak.

Alarmed by the mounting claims and counterclaims, as well as political controversies that grew in the capitals of Washington, D.C., and New Delhi, both Union Carbide and the Indian government took the path of least resistance. They decided the case out of court in February 1989 and arranged for the Indian Supreme Court to give its stamp of approval to a $470 million settlement, the largest such settlement in Indian history but far below the $3 billion the government initially wanted. It is still not clear how and why both sides agreed to the figure of $470 million.

Rather than providing a sense of closure to victims, the settlement was the beginning of a prolonged bureaucratic and political struggle, marked by large-scale corruption, to determine just who should get the money. Victims were outraged that a trial had been prevented—and thus a public determination of guilt. Real victims, often illiterate and incapable of understanding the byzantine bureaucratic system set up for compensation, lacked the "proof" that they were victims: evidence of treatment immediately following the disaster. Others who had not suffered paid bribes to doctors to get such evidence and thus qualified for compensation.

The net result of all this political maneuvering was to delay payment of settlements to victims who really needed the money and to create the widespread belief that the entire process of compensation was corrupt and justice therefore had not been served. By 2004, the officially recognized victims had received $1,000 each (in most cases, minus large bribes paid to officials to get registered as victims). Many in the West and among privileged Indians claimed that $1,000, by the impoverished standards of the victims, was more than generous. Warren Anderson, the CEO of Union Carbide, was convicted in absentia in the Indian court of "culpable homicide," the equivalent of manslaughter, but India never insisted on his extradition to face Indian jail time. In March 2000, he went into hiding (again) to avoid being served a summons in a civil lawsuit against him in the American courts filed by some Bhopal victims.

The Indian courts have never established a cause for the accident, beyond the basic fact that water mixed with nearly 50 tons of MIC on the morning of December 3, 1984, and triggered the runaway chemical reaction. Popular beliefs, of course, are an entirely different matter. In the summer of 2008, many Bhopal residents continued to believe that Union Carbide had caused the disaster as part of a secret chemical weapons experiment, just as Union Carbide's successor, Dow Chemical, continues to maintain the "sabotage" theory. In the summer of 2008, Bhopal remained deeply and bitterly divided. The absence of a formal legal admission of guilt stands in stark contrast to the case of Minamata. Unlike Union Carbide or the Indian government, the Chisso Corporation and the Japanese government both publicly admitted their guilt for the Minamata poisoning. Perhaps for that reason, Japanese society enjoys a measure of closure in the Minamata case that is visibly and painfully absent in the Bhopal gas tragedy.

A SILVER LINING?

If the Bhopal tragedy stands out as an extreme example of environmental injustice, there have been positive results. In response to the disaster, a plethora of organizations have given voice to formerly voiceless groups, including illiterate residents of the slums, the Muslim underclass of the shantytown around the plant, and especially women. These grassroots organizations are a testimonial to the vibrancy of Indian democracy (and differ, as the next case study illustrates, from the almost total absence of grassroots responses immediately after the Chernobyl accident). As in Love Canal and Minamata, many women in Bhopal found a political and social voice in the aftermath of the tragedy, a particularly striking development given the predominately Muslim character of the slums around the plant. For example, women took a lead role in marches, managed numerous victims' rights groups, and have established networks to build a broader environmental justice movement on the basis of their own experiences as Bhopal gas victims. The prominence of women contrasts markedly with the near invisibility of poor Muslim women in public or political roles in Bhopal before the disaster.

Rasheeda Bee was one of the most prominent activists. She witnessed six of her family members suffocate in front of her on that tragic December night in 1984. She noted that the disaster not only devastated Bhopal citizens physically but in the immediate aftermath the economy also came to a standstill. Many male breadwinners had died or become invalids as a result of the gas leak. Proud and determined, she said she faced a decision in the months after the disaster. "As a Muslim woman," she could stay in her shanty and suffer in silence. Or she could take a chance and embrace a new identity and leave her home. "Either I would do something or I would die." Through the 1990s, she focused on gathering money and aid for the physically deformed children of victims and on cleaning up the toxic wastes that remained on the Union Carbide plant site. Using charitable donations from European and American organizations she created a clinic to treat the children of victims. She formed a women's survivor group and has been closely involved in efforts to provide poor women with income and work. Unable to speak English and with almost no formal education, her clinic by the summer of 2008 had become a focal point, not only for other victims but also for women's rights advocates in Bhopal and Central India.

In 2004, Rasheeda Bee won the Goldman Environmental Prize (known as the "alternative Nobel Prize"), an award she displayed proudly. She has used the money from that prize and other charities to launch the "Chingari Award for Women Against Corporate Crime," an award that encourages other women to replicate her own experience and gain a political voice. The award places the struggle against multinational corporations into three contexts: fighting discrimination toward women in India, struggling to ensure that the burdens of pollution are equitably distributed, and combating vestiges of colonialism in India's relationship to multinational corporations abroad (ironic since her organization is funded partly by American and European philanthropists, including corporate donors).

Not everyone, of course, has viewed Rasheeda's new public role in Bhopal so positively. A number of middle-class residents dismissed grassroots activists such as Rasheeda as troublemakers and opportunists. As with Lois Gibbs in Love Canal, many locals challenged her motives, attributing her activism to a desire to become famous and stand out. Even within her own community, among men and other activists, Rasheeda's success has provoked envy and condemnation, especially her acceptance of foreign support, a politically explosive charge in Bhopal, where accepting foreign money invites the accusation of being a sellout to international corporate interests.[10]

THE DISASTER INDUSTRY

By the summer of 2008, there had also emerged an elaborate state infrastructure of medical care for victims, suggesting a curious disconnection between heated activist rhetoric about government neglect and the reality on the ground. Since the late 1990s, nearly a dozen new clinics and hospitals have been built to serve the victims, all funded by a trust formed from Union Carbide compensation money. "This is the silver lining of the disaster," said one medical bureaucrat in July 2008, beaming widely as he recounted the many new medical facilities in Bhopal that have resulted from the tragedy.

---

[10]Interview with Rasheeda Bee conducted by author on July 8, 2008, Bhopal, India.

It was a claim often repeated by many medical professionals and bureaucrats in Bhopal.

At the same time, international charitable organizations and groups such as Greenpeace have put together an alternative infrastructure of medical care and economic rehabilitation for the victims. They condemn the corporate system of health care as impersonal— and ultimately, as a reproduction of the hierarchical, corporate system of high-tech enterprise that made Bhopal citizens victims in the first place. Many critics of the official health treatment network aim to use an "indigenous system of medicine using herbal remedies to help the body heal itself," including Hindu techniques of yoga and allopathic medicines (viewed skeptically, it should be noted, by the majority of poor Muslim sufferers in the tragedy). Embracing a kind of alternative globalization, nongovernmental organizations from the United States and Western Europe have worked with educated Indians and local victim activists to create an alternative center of medical care in the heart of the Bhopal slums. Known as the "Sambhavna Trust Clinic," the operation moved into a large new complex in 2005 in the heart of the worst-affected Bhopal slums. The rusting remains of the Union Carbide factory loom ominously in the background a half mile away.

On surveying the vast infrastructure of victim care in Bhopal, one gets the impression that so many people now live off the tragedy that the actual impact of the disaster on human health is beside the point. In Bhopal, as in the other communities of this study, the disaster destroyed an old community, but it also created a new one based on a shared sense of victimization. Many Indian politicians and activists have skillfully turned the suffering of Bhopal into political and, in some cases, economic capital. Regardless of political orientation, whether one is pro- or antigovernment, the tragedy has become a lucrative industry. Even tour operators, for a time, exploited the disaster, offering European tourists rides in air-conditioned buses around the slums of Bhopal.

In the meantime, many people on all sides seemed to have lost sight of the actual suffering of the victims. One Bhopal politician in July 2008 proposed expanding the definition of areas affected by the disaster to an additional 20 wards within the city, thus ensuring that his constituents would receive payments as victims of the disaster. The politicians in the areas already designated as gas disaster areas cried foul, fearful that the expanded designation would lessen payments to their constituents. Others wondered if it was good for India's future to have nearly an entire city's population designated as "victims" dependent on handouts from the state—almost a quarter century after the leak. Wouldn't that cheapen the suffering of the supposedly real victims?

Debates over cleaning up the remaining 420 kilotons of toxic wastes at the former Union Carbide plant provide another case in point. In the summer of 2008, bags of toxic chemicals and mounds of toxic sludge were overgrown with weeds and trees, home to cows and the homeless, but essentially untouched since the night of the disaster. With every summer monsoon season that brings with it heavy rains, the chemicals strewn all about the area leach into the surrounding water systems that supply drinking water to thousands of residents in Bhopal's slums, slowly poisoning those not already poisoned by the gas leak in 1984. More than fifty victims and activists in the summer of 2008 staged a protest march from Bhopal to New Delhi, where they set up an encampment outside the seat of India's government.

Dow Chemical, which bought the remains of Union Carbide in 2001, has refused any responsibility for cleaning up the site, claiming that Union Carbide's earlier settlements covered its liability for the disaster. The problem, said the company, belonged to the Indian government, which seized the Indian assets of Union Carbide to build hospitals. In doing so, it took possession of the Union Carbide site and thus responsibility for its cleanup. The Indian government, meanwhile, in a rare instance when it agreed with many radical activists in Bhopal, has argued that Dow Chemical must clean up the waste and haul it back to the United States—to be dumped, no doubt, somewhere near a place like Love Canal. An Indian billionaire in 2008 offered to clean up the site, but Bhopal victims groups and the Indian central government rejected the offer. One group of Bhopal activists insisted that Dow Chemical clean up the toxic wastes and filed a suit in court to prevent the state government from remediating the site. Union Carbide created the mess, and Dow Chemical must clean it up, they argued. Never mind that until Dow cleans it up (hardly likely) the toxic wastes will continue to kill Bhopal residents. The political utility of the toxic waste problem in Bhopal, as often has been the case, took precedence over the suffering of the victims.

SOURCES

■ **Profit at All Costs?**

A U.S. Congressional hearing on Bhopal, held just nine days after the disaster on December 11, 1984, in Washington D.C., underscored the global nature of the Bhopal disaster. Like a Tsunami, what happened in Bhopal reverberated all the way to the shores of the Atlantic and up the Potomac River to Washington, D.C. Two factors drove Washington's interest in Bhopal. First, it was clear that Union Carbide, a U.S.-based corporation with powerful allies and lobbyists in the Capitol, was facing a public relations and potential legal nightmare that could severely damage the company's bottom line—at a time when the chemical giant was already facing financial troubles. Second, India was a key battleground in the Cold War. Since India's emergence as an independent state after World War II, the Soviet Union and the United States had fought a constant battle for the hearts, minds, resources, and loyalties of the Indian government. Both sent technical advisors, industrial equipment, and money to India to help the country industrialize. Both claimed to represent the only viable path to development. Both claimed a superior command of science and technology to legitimate themselves before the Indian government. Since the Bhopal plant ultimately belonged to the American capitalist side in the Cold War, the disaster at Bhopal constituted a major setback for the United States in the Cold War, just as Chernobyl, less than two years later, was a dramatic blow for Soviet prestige around the world. An intensification of the Cold War by Ronald Reagan, who in 1983 had referred to the Soviet Union as the evil empire, also raised the political stakes. Now many around the world could point to Bhopal as proof that the United States was the truly evil empire—a sponsor of toxic terrorism. For instance, six days after the disaster, the Soviet news agency TASS concluded that Bhopal was the inevitable by-product of a criminal policy of "profit at all costs" by Western businesses—and supported by their lackey political stooges in Washington, D.C.

Source: The Implications of the Industrial Disaster in Bhopal, India. Hearing Before the Subcommittee on Asian and Public Affairs of the Committee on Foreign Affairs. House of Representatives. Ninety-Eight Congress, December 12, 1985 (Washington, D.C.: U.S. Government Printing Office, 1985).

The following document consists of two excerpts from hearings that were held by the House of Representatives Committee on Foreign Affairs on December 12, 1984. Officials from the U.S. Department of State, Union Carbide, and an official from the World Resources Institute (an environmental think tank based in Washington, D.C.) came to speak before the committee and answer questions. As you read the following two excerpts (the first from a representative of the U.S. Department of State and the second from the Union Carbide's chief lobbyist in Washington, D.C.), identify the various implications of the Bhopal disaster. What legal issues did the disaster raise? Based on the questions and answers, what problems do you think multinational corporations posed for regulators in national governments? What was at stake for the United States—politically and economically? What do those answers tell you about the way multinational corporations, based in the United States, operated in other parts of the world?

Robert A. Peck, Deputy Assistant Secretary, Bureau of Near Eastern and South Asian Affairs, Department of State, responds to questions from the House of Representatives Committee on Foreign Affairs.

Committee member Solarz: Is anyone here from the administration today in a position to testify as to whether the safety and environmental standards in India with respect to this plant in Bhopal were less strict than the comparable environmental and safety standards with respect to similar facilities in our own country, or whether they were comparable to the regulations we have here?
Mr. Peck: No, sir, we do not have that expertise available now.

Committee member Solarz: I gather we have no extraterritorial application of American environmental law to the operation of American corporations or subsidiaries doing business abroad?
Mr. Peck: Generally that is the case, yes, sir.

Committee member Solarz: Let me ask you a question of national policy. If we come to the conclusion that an American firm is engaged in a potentially hazardous enterprise abroad, and if we determine that the safety and health and environmental standards and regulations of the country in which that firm is doing business, or in which it proposes to do business, are substantially less than here in our own country, and that as a consequence of the inadequacies of the host country regulations, there is a potentially serious hazard to the health and the safety of the people of that country or those who live or work in the vicinity of the facility, do you think we have any kind of obligation here to . . . restrict the operations of that subsidiary . . . ? Or do we take a kind of laissez-faire attitude and say . . . that is their problem, not ours . . . their responsibility, not our responsibility? Do you think we have a larger responsibility here . . . to impose certain restrictions and requirements on . . . American multinationals doing business abroad . . . ?

Mr. Peck: Let me say, Mr. Chairman, that we do not have a general policy today to exert that kind of control.

Mr. Solarz: I gather from what you said . . . that American companies are perfectly free to operate foreign plants . . . abroad . . . without regard to regulatory controls required in this country. Is that the case?

Mr. Peck: That is generally the case, sir.

Ronald Wisehart, vice president for Government Relations, Union Carbide Corp., responds to questions from the committee.

Committee member Solarz: Would you agree that you have . . . the kind of moral obligation to meet the highest [safety] standard possible, regardless of whether it is required by the host country law or not?

Mr. Wisehhart: Well, I think the record of Carbide and of the whole chemical industry indicates . . . the chemical industry is the safest industry in the United States.

Committee member Torricelli: . . . it is my understanding that in fact in India there are no provisions in the law for class action suits. It is also my understanding that there is no strict liability under Indian law. And it is also my understanding that there is a $300 filing fee for an individual claim, which of course is larger than the annual income of almost all the people who are affected in the area. And there are no provisions for waiving those fees under Indian law . . . that would mean for all practical purposes the affected thousands of citizens in India, and their heirs have no recourse in India under current law, meaning that their only opportunity for compensation is in the courts of the United States. . . . I wonder . . . whether your company would in fact oppose jurisdiction requests for the courts of the United States?

Mr. Wisehart: . . . we cannot answer this.

Committee member Torricelli: You are vice president of a company, and no doubt influence policy in the company. Wouldn't it be your own personal moral judgment that it would be an error to try to stop jurisdiction? That, in fact, there is no legal resource for the victims in India? The only assets that could be found . . . were in the United States, would that be your personal moral judgment?

Mr. Wisehart: I really don't know.

◼ Safety First?

Once a disaster ends, the blame game begins, as various interested parties (government officials, workers, and corporate officials) attempt to fix blame—and receive (or avoid paying) compensation. Within a week of the accident, lawyers for victims filed the first of many lawsuits in U.S. and Indian courts. Invariably, however, those with the most resources—Union Carbide in this instance—had the advantage. Union Carbide staged press conferences and used public relations officials to push stories in the media and vilify the victims, and it put lobbyists in both India and the United States into action. One study found that by far and away the most cited sources by American newspapers—and to a lesser degree Indian newspapers—were Union Carbide officials and American government officials. When it came to communicating and interpreting the disaster, Union Carbide controlled the message. Union Carbide, for instance, initially blamed the accident on worker sabotage—a disgruntled worker according to some accounts and in others a Sikh separatist with an agenda of independence from India. The account, despite the absence of evidence, was dutifully reported in numerous media outlets and Union Carbide continually promoted the "sabotage" theory in its legal defense. Rarely did mainstream American or Indian news accounts cite workers, victims, local officials, or doctors.

The truth about the accident, however, was far more complex—and damning, at least from Union Carbide's position. Union Carbide's pesticide operations, which were part of the company's agricultural products division, were losing money. The company had

Source: Excerpts of interviews with Union Carbide workers in Bhopal, published in 1994: T. R. Chouhan and Others, *Bhopal: The Inside Story. Carbide Workers Speak Out on the World's Worst Industrial Disaster* (New York: Apex Press, 1994), 86, 90–93, 94–96.

engaged in relentless cost-cutting measures, and the Bhopal plant itself was for sale. According to the calculus of most corporations, safety was figured as a cost—and not a benefit. And so safety became a secondary concern, as suggested by a 1982 internal Union Carbide safety inspection report, which emerged only years after the accident. The report noted that "operator turnover appears to pose a serious problem in the plant. . . . personnel were being released for independent operation without having gained sufficient understanding of safer operator procedures . . . there is some question about the adequacy of the tank relief valve to relieve a run-away reaction . . . no water spray protection has been provided or vapour cloud suppression in the MIC . . . storage areas."[11] This information was almost completely absent in versions of the disaster that emerged in the weeks after the accident. It took much longer for a more balanced account to emerge—one that included the point of view of victims and workers rather than press releases from Union Carbide and government officials. The following document contains excerpts from Bhopal workers who were interviewed after the accident. Their account was published only in 1994.

Why do you think that it took so long for the worker's version of the disaster to emerge? What picture of the workplace emerges from the testimony?

About September 1983, I was sent to the MIC unit for on-the-job training. There they told me that I must learn about the MIC plant from my fellow workers. When the plant was running, it was difficult to take on-the-job training, but somehow I began to learn about the MIC process. My demands for assistance were always refused. . . .

I joined Union Carbide on 5 November 1979. . . . During a one-year training period, I was given two months of classroom training and three months of on-the-job training; and in the remaining seven months, I worked as a regular operator, per management orders. The plant was ready to start but there was a shortage of trained manpower. Trainees were thus used as operators but only paid the wage of a trainee. . . . The treatment of operators by management was in all ways similar to unskilled workers . . . nine of my colleagues had resigned by December 1984 due to bad treatment by management,

---

[11]Internal Union Carbide memorandum, "Action Plan—Operational Safety Survey, May 1982." I found a copy of the document in the library of the Sambhavna Trust Clinic, Bhopal, India.

dangerous working conditions and lack of job security. . . . In my plant, there was no alarm system for automatic detection of a carbon-monoxide leak. . . . Leaks were common . . . I was, along with my colleagues, exposed to various chemicals . . . Initially, our factory had a loud siren and a public announcement system to warn outside public and plant personnel, but in 1983, our management modified the loud siren into a muted siren [which] could not be heard outside the plant. . . .

I joined Union Carbide in 1978 . . . Chemical leaks were common . . . throughout the plant. I was repeatedly exposed to various chemicals . . . The facilities provided for worker safety were not sufficient; even work clothes were not provided. [Right before the disaster as] we heard about the corroded pipelines, faulty pumps and valves, faulty instruments and gauges and untrained personnel in the MIC plant, there was more and more panic among us. . . .

I joined the Union Carbide . . . plant in 1973 . . . management only provided me soap and a cotton mask as safety equipment. No clothes were provided to protect me from toxic dust particles. When I went home, my family could clearly smell the insecticides. . . . There was no job security; any demand for extra safety led to warnings that we would be terminated. . . .

I joined Union Carbide . . . 28 March 1977. . . . They started training first in the classroom for two months without ever providing individual copies of the process and safety manuals.

■ **A Medical Professional's Perspective**

Dr. N. P. Misra, Emeritus Professor of Medicine, Gandhi Medical College, Bhopal, Physician, Governor of Madhya Pradesh, was the Dean of the Gandhi Medical College in Bhopal at the time of the Bhopal tragedy. He directed medical services in the aftermath of the disaster. He also was the chief investigator on the effects of the Bhopal leak for the Indian Council of Medical Research and he testified in New York City on behalf of the Indian government in 1986. His testimony was a centerpiece of the Indian government's legal argument that the case against Union Carbide should be tried in U.S. rather than Indian courts—a strategy based on the assumption that U.S. courts would award higher damages than Indian courts. The Indian government lost that argument. Dr. Misra provided the

---

Source: Interview conducted by the author in Bhopal with Dr. N. P. Misra, July 10, 2008.

following recollections on Bhopal in an interview conducted by this book's author.

[On the night of the disaster] I got a message at about midnight from some of the authorities of Union Carbide that the gas [methylisocyanate] has leaked and it is likely that some of the patients might come to your hospital for treatment. I asked [Union Carbide] what sort of toxicity studies they had carried out and what can you tell us about treatment. They had no information. . . . the only advice that [Union Carbide] gave me was that people should cover their face with a wet cloth. . . . But they had no idea about the toxicity except that it produces irritation to the respiratory system. We started getting patients by past midnight. They were very sick. They were having a lot of distress in breathing. Vomiting. Eyes were also red. And they seemed to be quite unwell. Because MIC is heavier [than air] it settled like a cloud over the area and engulfed all the people who were living there. I got two children who slept on a bed. One put his head outside his cover . . . he was affected by the gas. The other child was cold [and kept his head under the cover] and didn't get affected. . . . the leaves in the direction of the wind were totally charred and became yellow. And those that were away from the direction of the wind, nothing happened. I had another instance where the goods train [was stopped and] waiting to come into the station. All the cattle tried to run away from the gases. Those cattle which could cross to the other side [of the train] survived and those which were on the side [of the train facing the wind] all perished. I put tables and chairs around the roads we have at medical college and put some junior staff and students there to take care of these patients who come. . . . we put mattresses in the area which was available there . . . and on the roads. I knew that some of the persons might not reach the hospital. So I went across the street near Union Carbide and picked up people who were lying on the road . . . There were no ambulances available. There was no help from the other agencies. The total mortality that we recorded was approximately 400 for the first day which seems to be too meager concerning the episode, which involved approximately 200,000. Total deaths within the first 48 hours were approximately 2,000. I can't give you the exact figure. . . . we brought persons who were lying on the road. Medical examiners determined they were dead. So they were put in the morgue. Because we did not know the families who could come over and try and pick up these people we got them photographed and prepared a big sort of poster containing photographs of all these patients which were put not only in Bhopal but also in neighboring places. Some people never came [to claim the dead] . . . if the whole family perished there was nobody to claim them.

While Dr. Misra coordinated treatment of the victims, he also gathered data on the gas victims to be presented on behalf of the government of India in U.S. Federal Court. Dr. Misra recounts his encounter with the presiding U.S. Judge Keenan. In the following excerpt he recounts how he appealed to the judge's emotions. Why was this approach ultimately ineffective in swaying the judge's final opinion? Do you think the judge's rationale for not allowing the case to be heard in U.S. courts makes sense, even though Union Carbide is based in the United States and not India?

I presented the case on two consecutive days . . . and showed him about 600 slides. So I showed [Judge Keenan] about 600 slides which I carried with me from India to make him appreciate what had happened. . . . When I told him here are ten young children . . . can anybody ever compensate for their loss, that no amount of money can give them back the love and affection of their babies, he started weeping. [After he composed himself] he [asked] me who has advised me to come to New York for this case. This is not sound legal advice, he said. He said I will explain to you. You purchase a Ford car through their agents in Bombay. And that car meets with an accident because of some fault at the time of manufacturer. Where would you file a suit? In the United States or in India? I kept quiet. He said you do not want to speak but I will tell you I would file it in India. You have competent judges who can deal with these cases so why have you come here to present this case? I will throw it back to you. And he did. When I told my Prime Minister [about this], the late Rajiv Gandhi, he told me that this cannot happen . . . but I said the judge's remarks are final, he said that in this case the jurisdiction is not the United States, that you should try this case in India in the city where [this happened].

As you read the following excerpt, try to examine the tension between Dr. Misra's professional obligation as a medical professional and his legal role as an advocate for the Indian government's case against Union Carbide in U.S. courts. Were those two roles compatible? For instance, because Dr. Misra was testifying on behalf of the Indian government, he had to limit public remarks on the nature of the disease. At the same time, however, many victims and their advocates were upset that the government was withholding critical medical information—for supposedly nefarious reasons, many claimed, or to cover up the state's supposed complicity in the disaster.

[Those who claimed we deliberately withheld information] did not understand. The data was confidential, confidential because we were going through the court system. If the opposite party comes to know our data, they would misuse it and decrease the amount of compensation. Let me also tell you that I magnified the effects of the gas [to maximize compensation claims in the court] . . . But I said that most of these people who don't have symptoms today will have it tomorrow. And we will have a city of graves in Bhopal. That is the exact phrase I used although it is not true. . . . I knew that it was not [in order to get] maximum compensation. I told Rajiv Gandhi also that we must try to get an [out of court] settlement because if the court insists on asking me to prove each part of what I have said in the court I will not be able to do it. Well I said that many people will suffer from cancer. Almost all people who have been exposed will die, their life span will be shorter. So they must all be compensated according to that law of torts. But I said that if they ask for proof and they really argue it out, I would really not be able to prove it. It's very difficult [to prove such claims] because they will [ask] what is the scientific basis?

During his testimony in New York in 1986, Dr. Misra told the American judge that "Union Carbide owes a responsibility to . . . create a medical institution, a state of art medical institution and run it for the next twenty years." The comment initiated a discussion with Union Carbide and the Indian government over creation of a modern medical facility in Bhopal—the Bhopal Memorial Hospital, which was finally opened in 2000.

"[Following the accident, Union Carbide CEO Warren] Anderson met us and he was prepared to give us the money [for a hospital] and we were very sure that we would get this money. . . . but Rajiv Gandhi said nothing doing, we are not going to accept any money. [He refused the money because of] his sense of pride, that we are not going to accept anything as a gift from them who are the real culprits . . . [Gandhi] called me into his chamber in parliament, so I told him the case was likely to be shifted [to Indian courts] and I also mentioned about this money and he said, it can never happen and see that the case runs in the United States. Our prime minister was young, naïve and really did not understand the implications for courts. What should I do under these circumstances? I could understand the prime minister had not been able to appreciate what I had told him." Misra suggested a way out of the dilemma, which was ultimately followed—to confiscate the property of Union Carbide in India and sell it, "as a punishment from our side. Whatever money accrues out of that sale, that entire money should be used for medical compensation . . . so that's how this hospital came into being . . . I said there should be a silver lining out of this which is the hospital."

The resulting hospital is an impressive facility, but it is also a source of great controversy among many victims. Critics, meanwhile, have used charitable donations from around the world, without Union Carbide settlement money, which only goes toward modern medical facilities and practices, to create an alternative treatment center in the heart of the most affected slums of Bhopal. It provides alternative medicines—yoga, herbal remedies, and massages. Its creators are highly critical of the official government medical response as overly corporate, hierarchical, and ultimately dependent on charity from Union Carbide—the victimizer. Dr. Misra discussed his critics, those who provide alternative treatments to victims, as well as demands that the government initiate new health studies of victims. If you were a victim, how might you respond to Dr. Misra's statements?

[Those who advocate alternative treatment centers for victims] talk nonsense. They have no idea. They don't talk science. They talk fiction. There are hardly any victims left. There aren't any. Dead. They have all died. For more than 20 years. Those who are making noise, they want to get something out of that episode for themselves. And all these activists are living on money from various quarters and they want to survive. . . . You must differentiate the sickness that the common population has. Nowhere in the world are all people healthy. Otherwise there would not have been any necessity for hospitals. So there are sick people everywhere. We cannot differentiate if the gas is responsible for [later] deaths or if it is a natural thing. We set up [a study] to find out if there were high incidences of cancer in this population as compared to an equivalent population. There's no difference. It was a one-time exposure to a very noxious gas which produced an immediate effect and took a toll of human life and produced some type of irreparable damage in their lungs, eyes, and respiratory system . . . which can be classified as mild, moderate, and severe effects. Some of them could be treated but others who had severe irreparable damage, they could not be treated and they died over the years as a consequence. Those who had mild [exposure] have recovered completely. Those who had moderate [exposure] have got some respiratory problems but not so severe as to kill them. We followed up all pregnant people to see if there are any changes. There is an incidence of 9 per 1000 of congenital malformation in the newborn babies all the world over, even in the United States . . . [the incidence of congenital malformation in Bhopal] is statistically insignificant. We have subjected our material to great statistical analysis. [Those who criticize our medical care and research] are stupid, fools. They don't understand. That is a crude way of putting it. There's no scope for further research . . . Research means funding, full funding. Then it should be productive.

While Dr. Misra sympathizes with the patients, he categorically rejects the claim by many activists that compensation has been grossly inadequate or unjust.

[The compensation amount] seems to be [fair]. But as I said, any amount of compensation, given that it was none of their fault, is not enough. If you are working in a factory and you get your hand amputated, you know that you are exposed to that risk. Or you are working as a driver and you meet with an accident, and the government compensates you, you know the dangers . . . that is different. Those people were totally innocent from that point of view of the injured, so no amount of compensation will be adequate. But whatever has been given seems to be fair . . . they got their medical care, they also got their social rehabilitation. They also got some money.

Like many in Bhopal, Dr. Misra questioned the motives of those who continue to demand more compensation.

There can be two motives in this. One is to get more money by exaggeration knowing full well that these are not a consequence of the disaster. The second is that some people who have really been affected by gas they feel helpless and they want to get something more. And as I told you no amount of compensation would be adequate for that. Some people who have been exposed to gas may still be suffering. The majority of those seriously affected have died. Human beings are so demanding. Whatever you might do for them, they will not be happy. In our culture we say the happiest person is one who is fully satisfied with whatever he has got because he believes it is given by god and so he should accept it. Otherwise they will always go and complain . . . Everyone got compensation.

[Grassroots organizations and NGOs] have created a lot of nuisance. And they are still continuing to do this. They have dubbed me as a Union Carbide agent . . . They went to the chief minister to prevent me from going [to testify in the United States on behalf of the Indian government against Union Carbide]. I had a relationship with Union Carbide because they wanted me to conduct scientific investigations . . . I published papers out of that but that was for science. They also gave us in return . . . a lot of equipment. What was the harm of accepting a gift of equipment from them if they were going to give us a respiratory care unit?...So I don't deny that I had a good relationship with them but this does not mean that I will excuse them for this disaster.

Do you think Dr. Misra's relationship with Union Carbide compromised his objectivity—both as a medical researcher on the Bhopal gas tragedy and as a medical expert testifying in court—as many of his critics claim?

■ A Grassroots Perspective

Almost immediately following the accident, various activists began campaigns of sit-ins, marches, demonstrations, and legal appeals to force government bureaucrats and officials to address a myriad of concerns. Those efforts have continued unabated for more than two decades—focusing increasingly on the thousands of tons of toxic wastes left behind by Union Carbide at the site. The following text is an excerpt from a statement by Abdul Jabbar on December 3, 2004. Jabbar has campaigned on behalf of victims nearly nonstop since the accident. He is a fierce critic of the Indian government and he believes that Union Carbide has literally gotten away, and profited from, murder. Like many activists, he believes that there have been many conspiracies to silence the truth about the disaster. He refers to the accident as a "holocaust" and a "genocide," equating the Bhopal tragedy to the intentional dropping of atomic bombs on Hiroshima and Nagasaki by the United States in 1945. He also shares the widespread belief that the accident had been the result of a massive experiment on humans—a charge Dr. Misra dismissed as "stupid." Compare and contrast Mr. Jabbar's statements with those of

Source: Excerpts from Abdul Jabbar, "20th Anniversary of the Gas Tragedy," December 3, 2004. Mr. Jabbar provided me with a copy of the pamphlet in Bhopal in July 2008.

Dr. Misra. Whose position do you believe and why? How and why do the two draw such diametrically opposed views on the same accident? How would you reconcile these two radically different accounts? Do you think the metaphors of "holocaust" and "genocide" aptly describe the Bhopal tragedy?

During the gas leak, sirens of the factory were deliberately kept silent. While the city was dying, the doctors were totally clueless what to do. Carbide has not divulged the information about the impact of the gas on the human body. The company considers it a 'trade secret.' After the gas tragedy, the occurrence of lung tuberculosis in Bhopal is thrice the national average. In respiratory problems and cancer deaths, too, Bhopal far exceeds the national average, thanks to the gas leak. In the absence of information, doctors in Bhopal are still unaware of proper treatment of the gas-related diseases. Even the best treatment provides only temporary relief. The wanton use of steroids, antibiotics and psychotropic medicines has only aggravated the gas-related ailments. Inadequate treatment arrangement in Government sector hospitals has enabled business of private doctors to flourish. In the worst-affected areas, over 70 percent of the private doctors are unqualified quacks. Even the Bhopal Memorial Hospital Trust is as ignorant about treatment of the gas-hit as these quacks. In fact, a large number of medicines being provided by community health centres of the Trust are doing more harm than good to the old patients. . . . The hospital concentrates more on non-gas-affected and paying patients than the gas-affected in treatment. The hospitals meant to treat the gas victims have turned into dens of corruption where massive bungling has been going on in purchase of medicines and equipments with near impunity for years. While some mental and physical ailments had been afflicting the gas victims ever since the gas leak 20 years ago, some new complications have surfaced in the recent past. There has been an alarming growth in the number of deaths due to TB and cancer among the gas victims. The Government has miserably failed in treatment and monitoring of these diseases.

The official documentation of deaths due to the gas has been closed in 1992 even though deaths are still occurring. The callous neglect of the research and monitoring on the part of the Government has led people to wonder if it is due to the fact that most of the victims are poor people while those responsible for the tragedy are influential ones.

While closing down the factory in the immediate aftermath of the gas-leak, the Union Carbide management left behind a huge, untreated stockpile of poisonous chemicals, which include nearly 8000 metric tones of toxic effluent . . . and more than 10,000 tonnes of toxic silt . . . In

July 1998, the Union Carbide management handed over the factory to the Government of India and let the Government take care of the buried toxic stockpile.

Initially, the Government of India had claimed nearly 3 billion dollars on behalf of the gas victims for compensation. But the Government without taking the gas victims into confidence entered into a secret pact with the Union Carbide and agreed to the compensation package of 470 million dollars. [This amount] was grossly inadequate for the victims . . . Probably, they are cursed to remain afflicted for life. . . . The whole process of compensation distribution was steeped in deep corruption. As a result, a large number of claimants who were unable to bribe the concerned officials were deprived of the due compensation. Plus, there was no provision . . . for the mental trauma the gas victims have undergone. . . . Here it needs to be mentioned that for the kin of the victims of the terrorist strike at the World Trade Center minimum compensation fixed in each case is 16,000 dollars.

[The tragedy was] genocide and [Union Carbide used] humans as Guinea pigs to test poison . . . But no one has been punished. In order to save the accused, the company first fabricated a story of massive sabotage and then put the blame for the disaster on a disgruntled employee. Simultaneously, the company launched a campaign to steer itself and the top officials clear of the criminal culpability for the holocaust . . . the killer multinational company has managed to get rid of its responsibility of the worst industrial accident, taking advantage of the loopholes in the international laws, Indian judiciary and the executive setup.

We have been demanding construction of a memorial site at the Union Carbide site ever since the disaster occurred . . . These memorials would serve to caution our descendents of the holocaust much like the 'Concentration Camps' as memorials serve to remind about the terrifying face of the racial hatred that Hitler had unleashed in Germany. . . . The proposed memorial should be on a par with the ones at Hiroshima-Nagasaki.

■ The Controversy Continues

While Mr. Jabbar has been a prominent voice among activists, other groups have conducted similar campaigns. In the summer of 2008, one such group conducted a march from Bhopal to the parliament building of New Delhi—in imitation of the nonviolent demonstrations

Source: Excerpted from the pamphlet handed out at the demonstration in New Delhi, July 5, 2008, "Appeal to Stop the Bhopal Disaster."

conducted by Mahatma Gandhi against British injustice. Many activists were arrested in New Delhi, but eventually the fifty victims and activists were permitted to set up an encampment in New Delhi to remind the government and citizens, in their own words, "to stop the Bhopal disaster." Thus, nearly a quarter century after the accident, activists perceive Bhopal as an ongoing disaster—in contrast to the government, which has long since relegated the incident to the distant past. A brochure handed out by the demonstrators in New Delhi echoed many of Mr. Jabbar's claims, especially his belief that a continuing conspiracy has been responsible for preventing a just outcome for victims. If you were a citizen of India, how would you view the statements of the activists? What would you do if you were an Indian state official responsible for environmental protection? Does the statement provide evidence to substantiate its claims? Since the state stopped gathering health data on survivors or counting deaths from the disaster more than a decade ago, claiming that victims who later died passed away from causes other than gas exposure, how would one verify the figures cited below? Where do you think those figures came from? Do you trust these figures? Why or why not?

Over 23,000 people have died painful deaths [due to the Bhopal gas tragedy] . . . and today there are more than 100,000 survivors that continue to suffer from chronic illnesses. More than 25,000 people living next to the abandoned factory suffer a range of illnesses due to the contamination of drinking water by thousands of tonnes of toxic wastes from the factory. Most worrisome is the rise of cancers in the exposed populations and horrific birth defects among thousands of children born to gas exposed and toxic water exposed parents. Union Carbide Corporation . . . is absconding from the criminal case . . . The corporation was taken over in 2001 by another American multinational; the Dow Chemical Company. Dow Chemical refuses to pay for the clean up of the abandoned factory site in Bhopal, or produce its subsidiary Union Carbide in court in Bhopal. There is abundant documentary evidence that indicts the Indian government as an accomplice in the corporate crimes in Bhopal. In the last 23 years . . . the governments at the centre and the state have deliberately neglected the medical care and rehabilitation of the victims and turned a blind eye to the crimes of Union Carbide and Dow Chemical. The collusion between the American multinationals and the Indian government is the main reason why the Bhopal victims have been denied justice for the last 23 years . . . the government is helping these corporations escape their liabilities in Bhopal."

CHAPTER

4

The Techno-Politics of Disaster: Chernobyl and the Collapse of the Soviet Union

Early in the morning of April 26, 1986, operators botched a seemingly routine safety test on a nuclear reactor at Chernobyl. The reactor was located approximately 110 kilometers north of the city of Kiev, the Soviet Ukraine's largest city. The resulting steam explosion instantly destroyed the core of reactor number four, releasing at least one hundred times the combined radiation of both atom bombs dropped on Hiroshima and Nagasaki. A deadly radioactive plume soared into the jet stream and blew over Scandinavia—easily transgressing the political boundaries on the map, the so-called iron curtain that separated Eastern and Western Europe. Fireman and helicopter pilots dumped load after load of sand, lime, and dirt on the reactor core in a desperate and suicidal attempt to contain the disaster. It took three weeks to stop the emission of radiation. Dozens of the "liquidators," the term for firemen and soldiers who put out the raging fires, died agonizing deaths, as their skin melted away. They had to be buried in lead coffins to prevent their bodies from contaminating the earth in which they were interred. Millions of Soviet and non-Soviet citizens received massive doses of radiation.

Initially, the Soviets denied that the disaster had even happened—though U.S. spy satellites and radiation detection systems across Europe clearly indicated otherwise. Soviet denials put the lie to calls from Mikhail Gorbachev, the Soviet leader, for "new political thinking." Ludicrously clumsy attempts to cover up the accident seemed to confirm the commonly held view in the United States that the Soviet Union was an "evil empire," as President Ronald Reagan so described it in March 1983. Soviet Cold War propaganda compounded Gorbachev's dilemma. Soviet propagandists had crowed that operating a Soviet nuclear power plant (as opposed to the supposedly inferior American one) was as simple and safe as "stoking a coal furnace." They constantly reminded the world that the United States, unlike the Soviet Union, had experienced a near meltdown of a nuclear reactor at Three Mile Island in Pennsylvania in 1979. "Let the Atom be a Worker not a Soldier," read a huge billboard near the Chernobyl plant, repeating the frequent Soviet comparison of their peaceful nuclear power program to the atom bombs that the United States had dropped on Hiroshima and Nagasaki.

FIGURE 4.1 A Soviet technician checks toddler Katya Litvinova, in her mother's arms, during a radiation inspection of residents of the village of Kopylevo, near Kiev. (AP World Wide Photos)

So when the Chernobyl power plant exploded, far more than a nuclear power plant had been destroyed. Cold War politics, Soviet state authority, and technological mastery were inextricably intertwined at Chernobyl. Because the smooth operation of the political system, in effect, required the smooth operation of its nuclear power plants, the explosion of the reactor precipitated a profound political crisis from which the Soviet Union, and its leader Mikhail Gorbachev, may have never fully recovered.

ANATOMY OF AN ACCIDENT

To fully appreciate the impact of Chernobyl, it is important to keep in mind that the Soviet nuclear industry did double duty in nuclear and social engineering. The reactors produced energy, but they were also consciously designed to produce a new kind of Communist utopia. Pripyat, the city closest to the reactor, occupied the forefront of this complex techno-social mission—the Soviet fusion of physics and ideological imperatives. A young person's community of 45,000, Pripyat built and maintained the reactors, fulfilling the dictum of the Bolshevik revolutionary founder Vladimir Lenin: "Communism is Soviet power plus electrification of the entire country." A groundbreaking ceremony for the first building in Pripyat was conducted in 1970 with great pomp and fanfare. Soviet propagandists depicted nuclear reactors as temples of progress rising above the surrounding forests and swamps—the final act in the taming and domestication of nature. The "Atom City," as Pripyat was called by party hacks, had an amusement park with Ferris wheel, two-screen movie house, hotel, clubs, and a covered market. The Communist metropolis was filled with playgrounds, schools, and nurseries for the upwardly mobile Soviets who serviced and maintained the reactors. The nuclear physicists—the *fiziki* who produced the bombs that kept the United States at bay and the electrical power that fueled the Communist economy at home—occupied the highest rung in Pripyat. To land an apartment in the well-supplied city was the Soviet equivalent of the American dream. The average age of its residents in 1986 was just 26—and they embodied the youthful dynamism, technical competence, political loyalty, and energy that Soviet leaders hoped might spread to all areas of Soviet society.

A safety test, of all things, turned their Soviet dream into a toxic nightmare. Like all nuclear power plants, the reactor at Chernobyl produced power by splitting uranium atoms. The power generated from splitting the atom turned water in pipes around the reactor core into steam. The steam then spun massive turbines that poured electricity into the hungry Soviet power grid.

The purpose of the safety test on reactor number four was to disconnect the turbines from the reactor and use the kinetic energy from the spinning turbines to provide emergency power. The test attempted to solve a paradoxical problem: during an emergency shutdown of the reactor, there would be no power source for 40 seconds to maintain emergency systems—the time it took for diesel generators to restore power. Those emergency systems continually pumped cool water over the reactor and thus prevented the possibility of a runaway reaction in the reactor core.

When a skeleton crew for the night shift arrived, its members learned that their shift represented the last opportunity to conduct the trial before a scheduled maintenance shutdown of the reactor. They were apparently under intense pressure from political higher-ups. Due to an unexpected surge in power demand, the previous shift of operators had been forced to abort attempts earlier in the day to conduct the test. So they were determined, recklessly as it turned out, to complete the experiment.

Just past midnight on the morning of April 26, 1986, the crew reduced power levels in the reactor to 30 percent of their normal level, the planned level of power generation for conducting the test. They prepared to disconnect the turbines from the reactor and use the momentum of the spinning turbines for emergency power, much as a hybrid vehicle uses the energy from braking to recharge the battery engine. The operators then made the first in a series of fatal blunders: they inadvertently reduced reactor power to 1 percent of normal capacity. The rapid reduction in power produced xenon gas, known as reactor "poison." Xenon absorbs neutrons, which are used to split uranium and produce power. More xenon means fewer neutrons and thus a dramatic slowdown in the nuclear chain reaction. The production of xenon threatened to shut down the reactor completely—before the test could be completed. The panicked operators responded by pulling "control rods" all the way out of the reactor core. These control rods, like xenon, absorbed the neutrons that split the atoms. By pulling these control rods out of the reactor core, the operators hoped to increase the presence of neutrons and counteract the xenon, thereby increasing power production.

At this point the reactor was extremely unstable. The crew could only get the reactor up to 7 percent of its normal power-generating level. One analyst later compared the position of the unstable reactor to a car engine in which the driver simultaneously puts the gas and brake pedals to the floor. With each of the operator's panicked reactions came a new set of unanticipated problems. Because of the instability of the reactor, the normal automated water cooling systems did not operate correctly, threatening an automatic shutdown of the reactor that would have ended the test. To prevent that from happening, the operator shut off the automated water cooling system and, thus, one of the reactor's primary emergency fail-safe systems. Instead, he adjusted water flows manually, and incompetently, allowing excess water to flow into pipes surrounding the reactor.

Perhaps not coincidentally, many major technological failures, including the one in Bhopal, occur in the wee hours of the morning when personnel are less alert. At any rate, the operators apparently felt secure enough to conduct the test, disconnecting the turbines from the reactor at 1:23 A.M. As the turbines slowed, there was less power to direct cooling water over the fuel, as anticipated. Water in the reactor began to boil, producing steam and increasing the production of energy in the core, though not dramatically. At this point, the operator (for reasons that are unknown, since he died instantly) jammed the control rods all the way back into the reactor, perhaps resigned to the impossibility of conducting the test and initiating an action he thought would shut the reactor down once and for all. Regardless, he did not foresee the unintended consequence of his action. For a brief moment, the control rods displaced water at the bottom of the cavities into which they were inserted. That water, it turns out, had continued to absorb neutrons and slow down the splitting of uranium and production of energy. In a matter of seconds, the displacement of this water led to an explosive surge in energy to 10 times the normal power-generating level of the reactor. Water in surrounding pipes turned instantly into steam and blew up the pipes surrounding the reactor—a steam explosion that killed most of the crew, blew the 2,000-ton lid of the reactor into the air, and completely destroyed the reactor core. The force of the explosion belched out chunks of uranium and burning graphite through the 71-meter high roof of the reactor and onto the tops of adjacent buildings that housed the complex's other reactors. The steam explosion caused the release of radioactive materials directly into the air—like a great chimney ascending into the heavens and spewing forth radiation upon the surrounding earth.

POLITICAL FALLOUT AND HISTORICAL CONTEXT

Chernobyl could not have come at a more inopportune time—not that such disasters are ever opportune for political leaders. Mikhail Gorbachev had been in office for a little more than a year, replacing a series of frail and sickly leaders. Their enfeeblement reflected a more general enfeeblement in the Soviet political and economic system. The Red Army was bogged down in a disastrous war in Afghanistan—the Soviet "Vietnam." A dramatic drop in oil prices on the world market, the Soviet Union's main source of foreign income, had gravely aggravated a steadily eroding economic situation. If people had plenty of money, it was Monopoly money, since there was little of anything worth buying in the stores. As the common Soviet joke put it: "The state pretends to pay us and we pretend to work." When the 54-year-old Gorbachev ascended to the leadership position—General Secretary of the Communist Party—he thus launched a political and economic program called *perestroika*, or restructuring. He had an abiding faith that science and technology—and not free markets—would provide the energy, material resources, and intellectual firepower necessary to lift the Soviet system out of its seemingly terminal malaise. In February of 1986, he delivered a 5-hour speech at a critical party congress in order to consolidate support for his ambitious if vaguely outlined program of whole-scale change. And then, as Soviets were preparing for their biggest holiday—the May 1 celebration in honor of laborers, which Gorbachev planned to use as a launching point for his reform efforts—Chernobyl exploded.

Gorbachev and the Communist Party reacted very much as Stalin had reacted in the first weeks of the Nazi invasion in the summer of 1941. He was stunned and baffled and in a state of denial. The first impulse of the regime was to fall back on its business-as-usual habit of denial, obfuscation, and outright lies. As a matter of policy and practice, the state-controlled media (the only media allowed) did not report negative news about the Soviet system. Such reporting was considered a national security threat, for it would expose the system's weaknesses to foreign enemies. Since the late 1930s, newspaper editors were unable to report any domestic disaster, epidemic, airplane crash, toxic-waste leak, or large-scale technological failure. Such things, Soviets were told (and many believed), only happened in the West. Reading the long list of forbidden topics for Soviet editors—everything most people would consider "news"—one appreciates the challenge Soviet journalists faced in making sure the news went unreported.

While journalists maintained an awkward silence, the political leadership was far more concerned with maintaining secrecy and preventing panic than with treating victims. Immediately following the accident, a Soviet university instructor noticed that all books about radiation, even about x-rays, disappeared from the library shelves. Expert recommendations to warn residents not to drink milk, since it absorbed radioactive elements, were rejected because the authorities did not want to cause a panic. On May 8, 1986, a secret protocol from the Communist Party's Politburo, the Soviet system's ruling body, proclaimed: "The Ministry of Health of the USSR has adopted new levels of radiation which can be tolerated by the population, ten times higher than the former levels. In certain cases, these levels can be multiplied by 50."[1] By decree, tens of thousands of people were thus saved. In order to salvage irradiated meat, authorities mixed it in a ratio of 1:10 with normal meat and concocted sausages, hamburger cutlets, and meat dumplings. They assumed that diluting the radioactive meat and dispersing it as widely as possible in the USSR (the Soviet Union, after all, was a very big place) would harmlessly dissipate the contaminants. Such examples could be multiplied many times. They reflected the modus operandi of the system, its habit, in Orwellian fashion, of creating its own reality through bogus press reports, political decree, obfuscation, and lies.

Once the Soviet Union belatedly acknowledged the disaster (after nearly 48 hours and always erring on the side of downplaying the dangers), they mobilized manpower and heaved it at the enemy. They mobilized volunteers with stories of heroism and patriotic pride, consciously connecting the struggle against the burning reactor with the heroic defense of the Soviet motherland in World War II.

---

[1]Alla Yaroshinskaya, *Chernobyl: The Forbidden Truth*, trans. Michele Kahn and Julia Sallabank (Lincoln, Nebraska: University of Nebraska Press, 1995), 128.

Soviets had grown up on tales of heroic partisans and soldiers who martyred themselves to defend the Soviet Union from the Nazi scourge. Helicopter pilots and firemen arrived from all over the Soviet Union (many of them veterans of the Afghan war). They were enticed not only by the promise of greater pay but also by the opportunity to imitate the heroism of their fathers who had fought against Nazis in the Great Patriotic War (as World War II is known in Russia). There was a waiting list at the mines around Ukraine for volunteers to dig beneath the reactor and create a cement "sarcophagus" around the reactor. The firemen had a saying as they struggled to "liquidate" the disaster: "If not us, then who else?"

In the meantime, a secret protocol from the ruling Politburo, on June 4, 1986, established the official script that editors should use in reporting cleanup operations:

> When giving information on the progress of the clearing-up operation, demonstrate the efficient execution of large-scale technical and organizational measures which have no parallel in practice worldwide, to deal with the consequences of the accident and to prevent harm being caused by radioactivity; note the high level of mass heroism in the aforementioned work . . . Indicate the unjust character of the claims and judgments made both by certain prominent personages and by the press from certain Western countries, which speak of ecological and material damage caused by the spread of small quantities of radioactive matter carried by air from the Chernobyl area.[2]

While many liquidators sought glory and martyrdom according to the official party script, they also had little awareness of the dangers they faced. The pervasive system of censorship, which allowed only happy news about Soviet life, created a false sense of security for all—from Gorbachev at the very top of the system to the operators in the Chernobyl power plant. As the Russians like to say: "The fish rots from the head." The illusion of safety crippled the disaster response system, which had imagined that such disasters only happened in the West. The morning after the explosion, many

---

[2]Ibid., 132.

ordinary Soviets in Pripyat gazed at the strange emanation above the reactor, completely ignorant of the danger they faced. When the first fire trucks arrived, firemen discovered there was not a fire hydrant close enough to the burning reactor. City planners had not thought such a thing was necessary in utopia.

The heroic sacrifice of first responders, however, undoubtedly saved lives. Helicopter pilots dumped 5,000 tons of sand, lead, clay, and limestone onto the exposed core, as the firemen worked on the ground to put out burning embers of graphite. Despite official assurances of safety, many soon realized they faced certain death, yet they continued to work. On May 2, Soviet workers began building a concrete sarcophagus, entombing the exploded reactor in cement. Finally, three weeks after the explosion, the escape of nuclear materials had been contained. Firefighters had competed for the honor—a deadly one—to place a red Soviet flag atop the sarcophagus. The gesture linked the process of containment with the victory over the Nazis in World War II, when Soviet soldiers, after marching triumphantly into Berlin, placed a red flag on top of the German Reichstag on May 9, 1945. The liquidators had used 700,000 tons of steel and 400,000 tons of concrete to encase a mixture of approximately 200 tons of radioactive fuel, concrete, and sand—all of which had fused into a highly unstable radioactive mass under the intense heat of the initial explosion.

Among other things, the Chernobyl disaster showed that the physical world places limits on the human ability to fabricate reality. In one telling instance, the radiation of Chernobyl seeped into and destroyed the matrix of party mythologies and lies. The party had commissioned a documentary film to record the cleanup effort for posterity, casting the pilots and other liquidators in the role of heroic fighters for the Soviet motherland—effectively turning back the enemy of radiation to save the Soviet people and reaffirm the glory of the Soviet system. It was a familiar script, used thousands of times in movies and documentaries about the Great Patriotic War against the Nazis—or about any grave threat to the system. Due to the effects of the radiation, however, images in the film, shot from the helicopters working to contain the reactor, fade from the screen. The radiation spoiled the story, just as it contaminated 17 million acres of some of the Soviet Union's best farmland. Not even the most skilled editor and wordsmith could make that reality go away.

EVACUATION

Thirty-six hours after the accident, the authorities finally realized that people might have to be evacuated from "the zone." At first, they decided that people would be evacuated in a 10-kilometer ring around the reactor, an arbitrary decision based less on science than on a desire to show the world that the impact of the disaster was geographically limited. Tellingly, the initial order specified that cattle should be evacuated first—a dramatic illustration of the system's priorities and direct refutation of the government's supposed human-itarian impulses. The authorities soon expanded the zone, or *zona* in Russian, to a 30-kilometer ring. The process of evacuating more than 135,000 people from their homes was chaotic, brutal, sudden, and accompanied by a big lie: Residents were told they would be able to return in three days, when in fact they would never be able to return.

For many older residents, the improvised evacuation evoked memories of the panic that enveloped the area during the Nazi inva-sion of June 1941. Indeed, one common rumor at the time claimed that NATO forces had invaded from the west. Residents were not permitted to take even their pets out of the zone. Once the evacuees left, authorities hired local hunters to enter the zone and kill every pet cat and dog they could find. The pop, pop, pop of their guns fed rumors that militia men were shooting looters—though there is no evidence that such a thing occurred.

Little thought went into arrangements for the evacuees, since the authorities maintained the fiction that the evacuation was temporary. While many Soviets welcomed evacuees with generous offers of help and words of comfort (a story line that was endlessly repeated in the state-controlled media), others treated the "Chernobylites," as they came to be called, as a kind of leper colony. Evacuees were shunned and shamed, their children taunted and teased. Soviet newspapers, of course, omitted this aspect of the evacuation from their reporting. The absence of accurate information about the effects of radiation fed fantastic rumors about zombies within the zone and about the dangers posed by contact with a "Chernobylite."

While the Soviet press reported stories of heroism during the cleanup and evacuation, it ignored the many instances of prof-iteering, looting, and cruelty. In surrounding regions, as evacuees arrived by the busload, unscrupulous managers of grocery stores and gas stations held supplies from the shelves to create artificial shortages. They then sold precious supplies on the black market for a huge profit. Officials sold goods that were supposed to be distributed for free to evacuees at vastly inflated prices, making a tidy profit. Meanwhile, inside the zone, an informal process of recycling irradiated materials began almost immediately. In exchange for bribes, guards let people into the zone to seize items from evacuated residences. Corrupt officials worked with hired drivers to break into apartments and houses, steal the contents, and sell the items outside the zone—thus spreading irradiated household items across flea markets throughout the Soviet Union.

While many liquidators volunteered for duty in the zone, others had no choice. Soldiers and factory laborers were ordered by the busload into contaminated areas, armed with little more than a shovel and the clothes on their back. They jammed lead sheets into their underwear, hoping it would protect their private parts. After the initial radiation was contained, these liquidators focused on digging up and burying tons of contaminated topsoil across vast expanses of irradiated areas. Many of these laborers contributed to the black market for pilfered irradiated goods. Though alcohol was technically forbidden in the zone, illegal stills processed irradiated grain and potatoes into vast quantities of moonshine vodka, which workers in the zone believed would protect them from radiation. Liquidators drank copiously.

Once the city of Pripyat's 45,000 residents had been evacuated, teams of Geiger counter–toting men proceeded methodically through the city: 11 avenues, 3 banks, 10 restaurants and bars, 3 houses of culture with a movie theater and dance hall, 23 apartment buildings, and a police station with 2 drunk tanks. For months after the explosion, stop lights continued to cycle through red and green, even though the city was abandoned—except for lead-line armored vehicles and liquidators. Inhabitants had left their apartments in the middle of various activities. Meals were in various stages of preparation, clothes in wash basins, and drinks on the tables. The powerful stench of rotting food greeted the liquidators.

The showcase "Atom City" of Pripyat, like Love Canal, became a ghost town, a time capsule of the day the residents were told that they would only be leaving temporarily. In 2003, a journalist who visited Pripyat noticed that the clock above the community swimming pool was frozen in time. The hands did not move from 11:45. Chernobyl marked the end of Soviet time—and arguably of the Soviet version of progress.

One translation of the word "Chernobyl" in Ukrainian means "wormwood." The Bible's Book of Revelation mentions the burning bush of wormwood that will poison the waters and set into motion the Apocalypse at the end of history, the final battle between good and evil. Despite the Soviet regime's official atheism, many Soviets still remembered the biblical story of the End Times. If Soviet journalists earlier had treated "Atom City" as the fulfillment of Communist utopia, many ordinary Soviet citizens viewed the exploded reactor in a radically different context—as proof of God's existence. For those so inclined—and there were many within and outside the Soviet Union, including anti-communist Ukrainian nationalists—the immense concrete sarcophagus built around the reactor was less a strategy for containing radiation than a gravestone for the "blasphemous" Communist experiment.

THE BLAME GAME

As with all the case studies in this book, the immense scale of the disaster fed an intense desire to identify and punish the guilty party, a process sometimes referred to in disaster studies as "the blame game." Nearly every modern explanation of a disaster is typically packaged in technical language. Those explanations sometimes reveal true causes, but often they mask the political and economic interests of the powers that be. To understand the blame game, the historian should always consider the source and ask: Who benefits from a particular explanation? For example, official Soviet explanations overwhelmingly skewed toward absolving the system's political and technological leadership, blaming the accident instead on the incompetence of the operators. While perhaps at least partially true, the explanation was also politically expedient. It suggested that it was not the system that had failed—but a handful of incompetents.

To support the theory of "operator error," Soviet officials hastily arranged a trial less than a year after the accident. Conveniently for the prosecutors, most of the accused had died during or soon after the explosion, thus preventing any possible protest from many of the defendants. The proceeding was a classic Soviet show trial—less an exercise in legal argumentation or technical proof than a demonstration of a supposedly vigilant government's determination to catch and punish wrongdoers and internal enemies. By fixing blame on the operators, the trial also countered the explanation popular in the West (especially among the nuclear industry's lobbyists in Washington, D.C.) that the accident was the result of Soviet design flaws and not of the inherent danger of nuclear power.

The Soviet court's version of events provided a compelling and easily understandable explanation. The trial was a morality tale, with villains and scapegoats, enemies and heroes. The firemen, policemen, and party officials played the familiar role of the heroic Red Army vanquishing the enemy. The villains were mother nature, the atom out of control, and the operators, who played the familiar role of those vast numbers of "saboteurs" featured in earlier versions of Soviet show trials. The trial ultimately sent the message that things went terribly wrong because a few operators were out of control. The trial produced a guilty verdict for the few surviving operators, who were sentenced from 2 to 12 years in prison. Many Soviet citizens responded to the verdict by desecrating the graves of deceased operators. Whether they were dead or imprisoned, their family members were often ostracized.

The explanation afforded by the trial, however, was soon challenged. Events in 1991 in the Soviet Union created a strong tide of antigovernment sentiment in the population. The first democratically elected Soviet parliament—and the last before the collapse of the Soviet Union—established a special commission to revisit the problem of guilt in the Chernobyl disaster. It claimed that the operators had been scapegoats and that the real reason for the reactor explosion was a corrupt system, in which unelected leaders had allowed a dangerous and untested technology to be put into operation. In this version of events, the Communist Party and Soviet government were now on trial.

Five years after the accident, the Soviet Union had produced two competing official explanations for the accident. The judicial branch blamed the operators, and the newly democratic legislative branch in its investigation blamed design flaws and the Soviet leadership. Prosecutors from the Soviet Republics of Ukraine, Belarus, and Russia (all part of the Soviet Union) began preparing a new trial, which they hoped would reconcile these two positions. And then something totally unexpected occurred: The Soviet Union collapsed, officially dissolved in December 1991. Ukraine, Belarus, and the Russian Federation became separate nations. The prosecutor's office in Russia initially inherited the freshly reopened Chernobyl case, but the dramatic collapse of the Soviet Union completely overshadowed the Chernobyl investigation. Russian prosecutors argued that Chernobyl was not Russia's fault, but the fault of the collapsed government that had preceded it. Besides, Chernobyl, they added, was not in Russia but in the newly independent nation of Ukraine. The case expired with a whimper, as Russian prosecutors dropped it and handed over materials to Ukraine and the other affected new nation of Belarus. Both followed the lead of the newly independent Russian Federation, blaming the nonexistent Soviet Union for the disaster and dropping the case. Everyone had a convenient scapegoat—the defunct Soviet Union—which absolved any living entity, government, or person of responsibility.

TOWARD AN EXPLANATION

Definitive explanations are always hard to come by in complex technological failures, but most analysts believe the Chernobyl disaster resulted from a combination of operator error, technological design flaw, and a broader failure of the Soviet system of industrial management. The Chernobyl reactor had only a partial containment structure, so the design obviously played a role in allowing the massive spread of radiation after the explosion. At the same time, many reactors around the world have many of the same design features and have never suffered a catastrophic failure. The accident is therefore inconceivable without considering the actions of the operators—which, in turn, were a by-product of the Soviet culture of industrial management.

Since the 1930s, Soviet leaders had forced the pace of industrial and technological development. Acutely aware of Russia's backwardness relative to their enemies, they urged managers and workers alike to exceed production quotas in record time. ("Do the Five-Year Plan in Four" was a favorite phrase.) During the extreme emergency of World War II, in which the Soviets lost nearly 30 million lives, Soviet leaders became even more obsessed with rushing the pace of industrial development. Under pressure from political leaders, industrial managers made failure to meet quotas and fulfill orders a political crime, one that could get a person fired, thrown in jail, and even executed. The operators at Chernobyl thus grew up in a system in which political interference and commands were the norm, not the exception. A Soviet worker's job was to fulfill commands without question and as quickly as possible, and consequences be damned. Consider the fateful safety test. It had been delayed many times. It was clear to the operators that they had their last chance to complete the procedure—or else. They therefore rushed to complete the test, taking huge risks in the process. In the end, the operators feared the consequences of not completing the test more than they feared the possible disastrous consequences of the test itself, which probably had not crossed their minds until it was too late. In the context of the Soviet system of industrial management, which encouraged the fulfillment of orders at all costs, their actions made perfect sense.

The fear of questioning an order from above permeated the entire Soviet nuclear industry—and, indeed, the entire authoritarian, undemocratic Soviet culture. Tellingly, during a meeting in February 1986, just two months before the accident, one engineer said that work to start up a new nuclear power plant elsewhere in the Soviet Union had to be delayed because the necessary materials and safety procedures were not in place. A party boss exploded: "Well that's just great. Here's a man who sets his own deadlines. Who gave you . . . the right to set your own deadlines instead of the ones set by the government?"[3] The order-taking culture ultimately made it very difficult to challenge unwise orders from above, especially for the sake of safety concerns, which the leadership considered a cost to be reduced rather than a benefit to be maximized.

Rather than fostering critical thinking, the Soviet system of technical education focused on producing narrowly trained technicians, engineers trained in fields such as "the mechanics of rolled steel." Students in technical and scientific fields were not required to take general education courses in the liberal arts or to consider the ethical and moral implications of their work. Instructors focused instead on producing order takers, people who would do whatever it would take to get their job done—if that's what the bosses wanted. One nuclear energy official, who eventually committed suicide, commented after Chernobyl: "[O]ur school directs all its efforts to educating obedient, well-behaved and industrious boys and girls, little 'yes-people,' and does not educate in them a spirit of criticism. . . ."[4]

---

[3]Grigorii Medvedev, *The Truth About Chernobyl*, trans. Evelyn Rossiter (New York: Basic Books, 1991), 22.
[4]Iurii Shcherbak, *Chernobyl: A Documentary Story*, trans. Ian Press (New York: Macmillan, 1989) 148.

Finally, the disaster, and the system's equally disastrous response, stemmed from a failure of imagination (as was true to varying degrees in all four case studies) and not simply from a breakdown of technology. With the exception of a few dissenting views—whose opinions were never publicized—the Soviet system of technological management believed its own propaganda about the extreme safety of Soviet technology. It was a classic case of groupthink. Propaganda taught Soviets that nuclear accidents were a capitalist phenomenon and impossible in a socialist, Soviet context. The Soviets therefore treated the operation of a nuclear power plant in the Soviet Union as a routine affair, creating an illusion of safety that strengthened with every passing year of supposedly accident-free Soviet nuclear plant operation. For example, the pay for operators at Chernobyl was reduced to the same level as (or even below) that of operators at more conventional coal-fueled power plants. Managers assumed that the job of running a nuclear power plant was routine and thus required less skill and pay, echoing similar attitudes, incidentally, that contributed to the Bhopal explosion. The inability to imagine the full danger of nuclear power gave the operators a false sense of security on that fateful day of the disaster, and it also made Soviet authorities incapable of responding once the disaster happened.

CASUALTIES AND HEALTH CONSEQUENCES

Debates about the precise reasons for the disaster will no doubt continue, but the immediate toll of the disaster is undisputed: 47 pilots and firemen died a horrific death from acute radiation poisoning. The controversy surrounds long-term consequences. As in all the case studies of this book, the deliberate manipulation and suppression of health statistics, combined with the absence of systematically collected health data from people in contaminated regions, make it impossible to prove any prediction of future deaths or illnesses with any certainty. From the very beginning, doctors were under intense pressure from Communist Party bosses to minimize the scope of the disaster. That meant preventing doctors from getting information about the nature of the accident. Counterintelligence officials cut off telephone lines to Chernobyl (even for officials in the Ministry of Health) to prevent information from leaving or entering the zone.

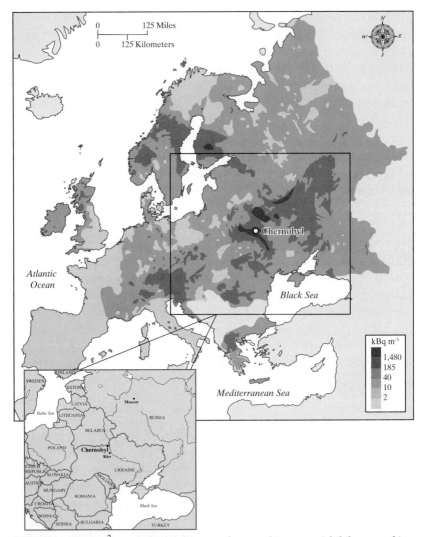

MAP 4.1   KBq m^{-3} stands for kilobecquerels per cubic meter. A kilobecquerel is a unit of radiation. The normal level for regions shown in the map before Chernobyl was about 1.5 kilobecquerels per square meter of soil. As the map indicates, levels of radiation in a number of countries surrounding Chernobyl (especially Belorus, Ukraine, and Russia) are still magnitudes higher than the norm.

The KGB warned health officials in Moscow to avoid "unpermitted" conversations (i.e., all conversations) about Chernobyl. They told them their phone lines were bugged and that revealing data about Chernobyl was tantamount to treason. Six months after the disaster, the Council of Ministers of the Soviet Union declared that all materials from investigations into Chernobyl were a national security secret. While the Soviet Union and the three successor states of Ukraine, Belarus, and Russia have commissioned hundreds of government health studies in affected areas, virtually nothing from these studies has ever been published.

The absence of published data gives each of the successor states plausible deniability regarding health damage from Chernobyl. For example, by 2004, Belarus (which received the brunt of Chernobyl's radiation) had taken 1,000 communities off the list of population centers endangered by radiation. It dramatically cut back compensation payments for victims (virtually worthless to begin with), citing the absence of negative health data as proof of the safety of these areas for human habitation. The Russian Federation and Ukraine have taken similar actions.

In the meantime, as the memory of Chernobyl fades, the international nuclear industry has minimized the long-term health impact of Chernobyl, arguing that Chernobyl was an isolated incident and pointing to the absence of a major nuclear disaster since Chernobyl. In September 2005, the International Atomic Energy Agency (IAEA) authored a report that predicted that no more than 4,000 people would eventually die as a result of various cancers and other diseases directly linked to Chernobyl radiation exposure. The figure is magnitudes smaller than most other estimates and almost exactly in line with official Soviet estimates in 1986. The report said that as of mid-2005, only 50 deaths could be attributed definitively to Chernobyl. The report claimed that there had been little need for the massive evacuations following the accident and for continuing restrictions on people moving back into evacuated areas. Echoing the position of pronuclear advocates in Russia, Ukraine, and Belarus, the report said that "persistent myths and misperceptions about the threat of radiation have resulted in 'paralyzing fatalism' among residents of affected areas." Chernobyl, it added, could not be directly connected to congenital deformations or instances of cancer. Poverty and alcoholism were far greater problems than radiation and should be the focus of health officials. Among locals, there was a widespread tendency "to attribute all health problems to radiation exposure," and as a result, many claim that health impacts from Chernobyl are worse than they really are. The report concluded: "The designation of the affected population as 'victims' rather than 'survivors' has led them to perceive themselves as helpless, weak and lacking control over their future." They suffer not from "real" ailments but from "self-perceived poor health."[5]

To the extent that such experts acknowledge increased rates of illness and death in affected areas, they attribute these statistics to supposedly "irrational" and hysterical fears of radiation, which produce a kind of antiplacebo effect, as well as outright fraud. The theory goes as follows. Subjected to supposedly relentless accounts of Chernobyl's disastrous impact, those living in affected areas have acquired a fatalistic view. Egged on by a supposed conspiracy of medical specialists on the make, people in affected areas have assumed a victim mentality, promoting various illnesses to get state handouts and allying with unscrupulous or unprofessional doctors and experts who, in the words of one pronuclear scientist, "force a healthy person to act ill, thus compelling him to feel ill and waste money on getting cured." Worst of all, feeling depressed and hopeless from all the bad news, residents near the reactor have taken up smoking and drinking to excess, thus creating the illnesses that they then attribute to Chernobyl. According to this type of analysis, which has become more or less the official position in Russia, Belarus, and Ukraine, the only effective solution to the Chernobyl legacy is a public relations campaign aimed at promoting the benefits of atomic power and at erasing the memory of the Chernobyl accident. The Web site for the Russian Atomic Energy Commission in 2008 presented a time line of events in the history of nuclear power. It does not include Chernobyl, though it does contain a cartoon for children extolling nuclear power as environment-friendly, efficient, and absolutely safe. It also contains a statement from Vladimir Putin, the Russian leader and former Soviet spy, that links the "glorious" history of nuclear power in Russia to the sacred mission of both the Russian Orthodox Church and the Russian state to secure Russia's land and soul: "Russian Orthodoxy and the nuclear industry are two themes closely related to each other because the traditional religion of the Russian Federation and the nuclear shield of Russia are those constituent components which strengthen the Russian state, creating the necessary conditions for guaranteeing foreign and domestic security. We can therefore conclude from this

---

[5]Joint News Release, WHO/IAEA/UNDP, "Chernobyl: The True Scale of the Accident. Twenty Years Later. A UN Report Provides Answers and Ways to Repair Lives," www.who.int/mediacentre/news/releases/2005/pr38/en/print.html (accessed January 30, 2008).

how the state in the future must relate to both."[6] The comments raise serious questions about how much state approaches to managing science and technology have changed since the collapse of the Soviet Union, at least in the Russian Federation. Based on this comment from the Russian leader, anyone criticizing nuclear power is not only opposed to Russian national security but also to God (in Soviet times, the Communist Party would have stood in God's position).

The tendency to downplay Chernobyl's negative impact—indeed, to completely erase its memory in favor of a "glorious" nuclear past—has coincided with a worldwide revival of the nuclear industry. It has also evoked howls of protest from environmental groups, especially Green Party activists in Europe. The Green Party representative in Europe in 2006 authored a report that was released in Kiev and titled "The Other Report on Chernobyl." It claimed that 40 percent of Europe's entire surface had been contaminated by Chernobyl. It predicted that at least 60,000 people would die from Chernobyl-related illnesses, 15 times the number predicted by the IAEA. It concluded that the IAEA report (supposedly in contrast to its own) was "a political document, intended to downplay [the Chernobyl disaster] . . . for the interests of the nuclear power industry."[7]

One thing is certain: The Soviet obsession with secrecy has greatly complicated any attempt to understand the actual threat posed by Chernobyl. This culture of secrecy has had debilitating psychological as well as political and health effects. Local governments today lack both the resources and the information they need to understand, much less respond to, the legacies of toxic contamination. Meanwhile, the realization of possible contamination, combined with the understanding that the truth can never be known, has created a constant state of stress among residents about their surrounding environment. People simply do not know the dangers they face living even hundreds of kilometers from the reactor, especially since the toxins that might inhabit their environment are invisible. Faced with the impossibility of knowing for sure, many who live in the contaminated zones, or who are responsible for governing them, conclude that the only solution is to simply stop talking about the problem and move on.

---

[6]http://museum.rosenergoatom.ru/index.wbp?bandwidth=low (accessed January 7, 2009).
[7]Nuclear Information & Resource Service, "New Study Challenges IAEA Report on Chernobyl Consequences: Finds Death Toll Likely to be 30–60,000," www.nirs.org/press/04-11-2006/1 (accessed January 30, 2008).

CHERNOBYL AFTER CHERNOBYL

Chernobyl in the twenty-first century is a city of guards, whose function is to maintain and protect the 30-kilomoter exclusion zone. A French engineering company has been hired to replace the cement sarcophagus, leaking and cracked and meant to last only 30 years, with a new metal structure. The appearance of fences and guards around the zone, however, is deceiving. Like all human-made fences, the borders of the exclusion zone are porous. Bribes can penetrate them, allowing humans to travel back and forth across the boundaries of the zone. Animals pass freely across the borders. Radiation continues to leak out of the zone—often in the form of timber and agricultural products produced, mostly illegally, on contaminated lands. In the first decade of the twenty-first century, approximately 4,000 people continued to work in and around the station itself. Another 3,000 from the "ministry of extreme situations," along with 600 or so policemen, guarded the area from intruders and brushfires—a common plague, often caused by arsonists, whose fires release the radioactive material absorbed by trees and plants. The population was almost exclusively male, served by one functioning post office, which in 2003 received an average of 60–80 pieces of mail a day, mostly pension checks for older residents who refused to leave their homes. Workers in 2003 worked two-week shifts—two weeks in and two weeks out—to avoid overexposure. A newspaper, called *The Chernobyl Gazette*, serviced the residents, along with one café. In 2003, the authorities gave up the attempt to make Chernobyl an alcohol-free zone. They began distributing vodka to workers every Tuesday—the day a new shift entered the zone. The residents, according to one source, averaged a half liter of vodka per day. Paradoxically, the natural world in the zone appears to be thriving, relieved of the relentless pressures of human civilization. Some scholars have referred to the seemingly pristine and natural view of Chernobyl (which masks an invisible but very real radioactive reality) as the "Chernobyl Paradox." Finally, Chernobyl has been, and remains, a fertile breeding ground for legends and rumors. The creation of the "exclusion zone," encased in barbed wire and existing in a kind of alternative universe, has made Chernobyl a mysterious and, for some, an enchanted space. One persistent legend that survived and grew after the disaster was that a missile radar locator 3 kilometers from the power plant, called Chernobyl-2, turned locals into zombies.

The presence of wobbly drunks within the zone, who struggle mightily to stay on the asphalt roads and walkways because they are less radiated than the earth, no doubt fed such legends.

SOURCES

■ A Misfortune Has Befallen Us

The following are excerpts from Gorbachev's first major speech about the accident, three weeks following the disaster. As you read, consider Chernobyl from Gorbachev's point of view. How does he try to minimize the political impact of Chernobyl? How does he try to spin the disaster in favor of Soviet political authority? Do you think he deals successfully with the political firestorm created by Chernobyl (the actual radiation, of course, is a different matter)? Based on this speech, how does the context of the Cold War with the United States influence Gorbachev's interpretation of the disaster and its aftermath?

Television Address by Mikhail Gorbachev, 14 May 1986, Moscow

Good evening, comrades. As you all know, a misfortune has befallen us—the accident at the Chernobyl nuclear power plant. . . . For the first time ever we have faced the reality of such a sinister force as nuclear energy out of control. Considering the extraordinary and dangerous nature of what had happened in Chernobyl the Political Bureau took charge of the entire organization of work to ensure that the breakdown was dealt with as speedily as possible and its consequences limited. . . . It goes without saying that when investigation of the causes of the accident is complete, all necessary conclusions will be drawn and measures will be taken to rule out repetition of anything of the sort. . . . In the situation that had arisen we considered it our top priority duty . . . to ensure the safety of the population and provide effective assistance to those who had been affected by the accident. . . . The inhabitants of the settlement near the power station were evacuated within a matter of hours and then, when it had

---

Source: The full translation of the speech from which this is excerpted is contained in Richard Mould, *Chernobyl: The Real Story* (New York: Pergamon Press, 1988), 195–201.

become clear that there was a potential threat to the health of people in the surrounding zone, they also were moved to safe areas. All this complicated work required the utmost speed, organization and precision. . . . The Soviet government will take care of the families of those who died and who were injured. The inhabitants of the areas that have cordially welcomed the evacuees deserve the highest appreciation. They responded to the misfortune of their neighbours as though it was their own, and in the best traditions of our people displayed consideration, responsiveness and attention. . . . A stern test has been and is being passed by all concerned, firemen, transport and building workers, medical personnel, special chemical protection units, helicopter crews and other detachments of the Ministry of Defence and Ministry of Internal Affairs. . . . I must say that people have acted and are continuing to act heroically, selflessly. I think we will have an opportunity later to name these courageous people and assess their exploits worthily. I have every reason to say that, despite the utter gravity of what happened, the damage has turned out to be limited. . . . Thanks to the effective measures taken, it is possible to say today that the worst is past. The most serious consequences have been avoided. . . . We are warmly appreciative of foreign scientists and specialists who have shown readiness to come up with assistance in overcoming the consequences of the accident. . . . But it is impossible to ignore and make no political assessment of the response to the event at Chernobyl by the governments, political figures and the mass media in certain NATO countries, especially the USA. They launched an unrestrained anti-Soviet campaign. It is difficult to imagine what was said and written then— "Thousands of Casualties," "Mass Graves of the Dead," "Desolate Kiev," "The Entire Land of the Ukraine Has Been Poisoned," and so on and so forth. Generally speaking, we faced a veritable mountain of lies—most dishonest and malicious lies. . . . What, in actual fact, was behind that highly immoral campaign? Its organizers, to be sure, were not interested in either true information about the accident or the fate of the people at Chernobyl . . . They needed a pretext to . . . lessen the impact of Soviet proposals on the termination of nuclear tests and on the elimination of nuclear weapons, and at the same time to dampen the growing criticism of US conduct on the international scene and its militaristic course. . . . The accident at the Chernobyl station and the reaction to it have become a kind of test of political morality. . . . The ruling circles of the USA and their most zealous allies—I would like to mention especially the Federal Republic of Germany—regarded the mishap only as another opportunity to put up additional obstacles holding back the development and deepening of the current East–West dialogue . . . to justify the nuclear arms race. . . . Everybody remembers that it took the US authorities ten days to inform their own congress and months to inform the world community about the tragedy that took place at Three Mile Island atomic power station in 1979. I have already said how we acted. All this enables one to judge who best approaches the matter of informing their own people and foreign countries. . . . The accident at Chernobyl showed again what an abyss will open if nuclear war befalls mankind. For inherent in the nuclear arsenals stockpiled are thousands upon thousands of disasters far more horrible than the Chernobyl one. Given the increased attention to nuclear matters, the Soviet Government, having considered all the circumstances connected with the safety of its people and the whole of humanity, has decided to extend its unilateral moratorium on nuclear tests until August 6 of this year, that is until the date on which, more than 40 years ago, the first atomic bomb was dropped on the Japanese city of Hiroshima, as a result of which hundreds of thousands of people perished. . . . Let those who are at the head of the United States show by deeds their concern for the life and health of people. I confirm my proposal to President Reagan to meet without delay in the capital of any European State that will be prepared to accept us or, say, in Hiroshima and to agree on a ban on nuclear testing.

■ The Western Nuclear-Power Industry Reacts

While Chernobyl precipitated a broad-ranging crisis in the Soviet Union, it also presented a grave challenge for the nuclear industry in the West. Cold War opponents of the Soviet Union wanted to exploit the disaster as proof of the superiority of the United States, but they also realized that the disaster threatened public acceptance of nuclear power more generally. The clearest expression of the position of the American nuclear industry and its advocates comes from a particular

Source: Ray Silver, "Nuclear Industries Craft Post-Chernobyl Public Relations Programs," *Nucleonics Week*, June 19, 1986, 9.

kind of source known as the "trade press." Most industries have a magazine or newsletter that publishes news of interest to those involved in the industry. The publications are supported by advertising from the businesses whose executives read them. Lobbyists and public relations officials are often featured on the pages of these publications. In the weeks and months following the accident, the pronuclear trade press was filled with articles containing headlines such as the following June 30, 1986, article in *Chemical and Engineering News*: "New Era of Inherently Safe Nuclear Reactor Technology Nears." The following document is excerpted from an article in the trade publication *Nucleonics Week*, a weekly newspaper devoted to promoting nuclear power. Titled "Nuclear Industries Craft Post-Chernobyl Public Relations Programs," it was published on June 19, 1986, less than two months after the disaster, based on comments from nuclear officials and executives at a conference in Toronto, Canada.

Western reactions to Chernobyl were not uniform. How and why did reactions differ? How did the officials and executives propose to counter the inevitable distrust of their industry that would follow news of this disaster? From what you know of the history of the industry following Chernobyl, were their efforts successful?

"We were on a roll until Chernobyl blew its top. There is no question that the Chernobyl accident had dealt us all an enormous setback," Carl Goldstein, vice-president of the U.S. Committee for Energy Awareness (CEA), told conference goers. "But even though public sentiment has turned sour, there is still a very strong inevitability factor in our favor." . . . Goldstein foresees a much longer, tougher period ahead now to restore public confidence. "Chernobyl is a chronic, rolling event. Reports will trickle out of the Soviet Union, and we'll be living with health effects studies for a long time," he said. Confident that the industry ultimately will be sustained by the public's "pragmatic attitude of nuclear power's inevitability," Goldstein said, "The public now recognizes that TMI [Three Mile Island] was almost a non-event," compared to Chernobyl. . . . Tom Margerison, director of the British industry's Nuclear Electricity Information Group (NEIG), said that they had not scrapped "fairly large-scale advertising plans based on the American program. New public relations and advertising programs will emphasize industry candidness, "absolute accuracy," and more humility. "It is very easy for people who are technically qualified to be arrogant in their dealings with the ignorant public . . . Attacking the Russians would not be good. It is better to say that the Russians are capable technologists but something must have gone wrong," he said. . . . British reaction to Chernobyl was more negative than in France but probably less so than in West Germany, he told *Nucleonics Week*. "The French have no gas, oil, coal, or choice. They have to use nuclear power. We are sitting on a lot of coal and the miners are opposed to closing the pits. North Sea oil is beginning to decline but we still have it. We are fossil-fuel rich and nuclear is a relative luxury for us. We don't have as militant an antinuclear group as the West German Green Party." . . . Basil A. Beneteau, a director of Atomic Energy of Canada, Ltd. and head of the federal government's task force on privatization of such crown corporations as Eldorado Nuclear Ltd., told the conference . . . , "the nuclear industry is here to stay . . . Canadians have shown a remarkable level of mistrust considering the safety, efficiency, and lack of pollution from Canada's nuclear plants. What the industry has not realized, and perhaps few could have guessed, is the strength of public mistrust and the need for sustained public education programs. Our critics have outgunned us. . . . Today's critics are more sophisticated. . . . They are taking their message to their elected representatives and public agencies. . . . Even when no one is being hurt, let alone killed, we are considered a threat because what is not understood is threatening. We need to make our technology seem familiar and commonplace; to take a lesson from the computer industry and learn to be 'user friendly.' "

■ The Myth of Chernobyl?

In the years since the disaster, increasing numbers of government and quasi-government officials have taken the position that the disaster was not nearly as bad as most think. The "complex" of myths and legends, as one book published in 2006 by a conservative Russian physicist put it, was the creation of anti-Soviet elements: "In the twenty years since Chernobyl I can't recall a single instance when the participation of civil society in government produced any good result." On the contrary, when it came to the nuclear industry, they had only stalled the completion of new power plants, thus needlessly wasting resources and stalling the production of power and jobs. "The Chernobyl catastrophe activated the activity of various nature protection organizations who received the ability to impose at will their neuroses on the population—and on political power. . . .

Source: N. N. Nepomniashchii, *Chernobyl: Neizvestnye podrobnosti katastrofy* [Chernobyl: Unknown Facts about the Disaster] (Moscow: Veche, 2006), 199–200.

Anti-scientific attitudes predominated—and Russia lost the prestige and power that came with technological prowess and mastery, all for the sake of a post-totalitarian . . . democracy."[8] The following are excerpts of statements from various experts in Ukraine and Poland who share such views—and whose comments are used in the Russian press and elsewhere to advance the notion that the accident has been greatly exaggerated for political and economic reasons.

What are their apparent motivations? Does their status as "experts" with advanced degrees make their claims more convincing? If you were an opponent of nuclear power, how might you challenge their claims? If you were a supporter of nuclear power, how might you use their expertise? Compare the scientific arguments made by Dr. Misra regarding the incidence of deaths following the Bhopal disaster and that of Academician Amosov. Both claim that there is no evidence that death rates following the disasters in Chernobyl and Bhopal were any higher than death rates that would have normally occurred absent the disasters. Does either seem convincing? Why or why not?

Nikolai Amosov, Academician, Ukrainian Academy of Sciences
Chernobyl—this is a problem exaggerated by writers and politicians. In Russia and in the Urals [before the Chernobyl disasters] there have been much more serious extreme situations. But Soviet authorities did not report this information. With Chernobyl it was different. It is a myth which medicine says hallelujah to because [the medical profession] lives at its expense. Out of 100,000 liquidators over fifteen years a few dozen have died. If you take the natural death rate over the same period, you would have something analogous to Chernobyl.

Dr. Mikhail Valigorski, chair of the department of physical medicine in Cracow
The Chernobyl refugees did not die from deadly dosages of radiation but from stress. We observed similar reactions to stress during the 1997 flood in Poland.

Professor Kazimezh Obukhovski, Institute of Psychology, Poland
The catastrophe occurred at a time when there was still a conflict between two nuclear powers and various organizations endlessly nattered on about the possible consequences of nuclear war. People awaited news which might confirm their fears and anxieties and considered [the Chernobyl catastrophe] just such a thing.

---

[8]Sergei Pereslegin, *Mify Chernobylia* [The Myths of Chernobyl] (Moscow, 2006), 73–74, 78.

■ Victims and Heroes: Voices from Chernobyl

Soviet press coverage of the disaster focused on the heroism of the firemen, helicopter pilots, and other liquidators, who sacrificed their health and often their lives to put out the fires and contain the radiation. In the official Soviet press coverage, the story of Chernobyl was the story of individual and communal sacrifice, efficient and effective government response, a caring political leadership—and the lies and cynicism of the Soviet Union's enemies. The reality, however, was different, as illustrated by a powerful collection of testimonials from eyewitnesses published in English under the title *Voices from Chernobyl.*

As you read the following excerpts, compare the official Soviet story to the experiences of the victims. Why do you think the first eyewitness finds it impossible to make sense out of Chernobyl? Consider the stories told by the liquidators. How do you think they would respond to those who would call them heroes? What motivated them? What do these stories reveal about the ideology and nature of Soviet society?

Yevgeniy Brovkin, instructor at Gomel State University, an area highly contaminated by Chernobyl radiation

I suddenly started wondering what's better—to remember or to forget? Some have forgotten, others don't want to remember, because we can't change anything anyway, we can't even leave here. Here's what I remember. In the first days after the accident, all the books at the library about radiation, about Hiroshima and Nagasaki, even about X-rays, disappeared. Some people said it was an order from above, so that people wouldn't panic. There was even a joke that if Chernobyl had blown up near the Papuans, the whole world would be frightened, but not the Papuans. There were no medical bulletins, no information. Those who could, got potassium iodide[9] (you couldn't get it at the pharmacy in our town, you had to really know someone). Some people took a whole bunch of those tablets and washed them down with liquor. They had to get their stomachs pumped at the hospital. Then we discovered a sign, which all of us followed: as long as there were sparrows and pigeons in town, humans could live there, too. I was in a taxi one time, the driver

---

Source: Svetlana Alexievich, *Voices from Chernobyl,* trans. Keith Gessen (New York: Picador, 2006), 84–86, 86–92, 44–45.
[9]A chemical agent that blocks the accumulation of radioactive iodine 131 in the thyroid gland. It does not protect against other forms of radiation poisoning.

couldn't understand why the birds were all crashing into his window, like they were blind. They'd gone crazy, or like they were committing suicide. I remember coming back one time from a business trip. There was a moonlit landscape. On both sides of the road, to the very horizon, stretched these fields covered in white dolomite. The poisoned topsoil had been removed and buried, and in its place they brought white dolomite sand. It was like not-earth. This vision tortured me for a long time and I tried to write a story. I imagined what would be here in a hundred years: a person, or something else, would be galloping along on all fours, throwing out its long back legs, knees bent. At night it could see with a third eye, and its only ear, on the crown of its head, could even hear how ants run. Ants would be the only thing left, everything else in heaven and earth would have died. I sent the story to a journal. They wrote back saying that this wasn't a work of literature, but the description of a nightmare. Of course, I lacked the talent. But there was another reason they didn't take it, I think. I've wondered why everyone was silent about Chernobyl, why our writers weren't writing much about it—they write about the war, or the camps, but here they're silent. Why? Do you think it's an accident? If we'd beaten Chernobyl, people would talk about it and write about it more. Or if we'd understood Chernobyl. But we don't know how to capture any meaning from it. We're not capable of it. We can't place it in our human experience or our human timeframe. So what's better, to remember or to forget?

****

[The following are stories from liquidators regarding their experiences in the contaminated zone, where they worked burying contaminated soil for half a year.]
I wasn't afraid to die, then. My wife didn't even send a letter. In six months, not a single letter. Want to hear a joke? This prisoner escapes from jail, and runs to the thirty-kilometer Zone at Chernobyl. They catch him, bring him to the dosimeters. He's "glowing" so much, they can't possibly put him back in prison, can't take him to the hospital, can't put him around people. Why aren't you laughing? When I got there, the birds were in their nests, and when I left the apples were lying on the snow. We didn't get a chance to bury all of them. We buried earth in the earth. With the bugs, spiders, leeches. . . . That's my most powerful impression of that place—those bugs. I haven't told you anything, really. Just snippets. . . . Leonid Andreev[10] has a parable about a man who lived in Jerusalem, past whose house Christ was taken, and he saw and heard everything, but his tooth hurt. He watched Christ fall while carrying the cross, watched him fall and cry

---

[10]Russian playwright and author of short stories who died in 1919.

out. He saw all of this, but his tooth hurt, so he didn't run outside. Two days later, when his tooth stopped hurting, people told him that Christ had risen, and he thought: "I could have been a witness to it. But my tooth hurt." Is that how it always is? My father defended Moscow in 1942. He only learned that he'd been part of a great event many years later, from books and films. His own memory of it was: "I sat in a trench. Shot my rifle. Got buried by an explosion. They dug me out half alive-alive." That's it. And back then, my wife left me.

****

They made the call, and I went. I had to! I was a member of the Party. Communists, march! That's how it was. I was a police officer—senior lieutenant. They promised me another "star." This was June 1987. You were supposed to get a physical, but they just sent me without it. Someone, you know, got off, brought a note from his doctor that he had an ulcer, and I went in his place . . . There were already jokes. Guy comes home from work, says to his wife, "They told me that tomorrow I either go to Chernobyl or hand in my Party card." "But you're not in the Party." "Right, so I'm wondering: how do I get a Party card by tomorrow morning?"

We went as soldiers, but at first they organized us into a masonry brigade. We built a pharmacy. Right away I felt weak and sleepy all the time. I told the doctor I was fine, it was just the heat. The cafeteria had meat, milk, sour cream from the collective farm, and we ate it all. The doctor didn't say anything. They'd make the food, he'd check with his book that everything was fine, but he never took any samples. We noticed that. That's how it was. We were desperate. Then the strawberries started coming and there was honey everywhere. The looters had already been there. . . . The stores were all looted, the grates on the windows broken in, flour and sugar on the floor, candy. . . . One village got evacuated, and then five to ten kilometers over, the next village didn't. . . . I spent six months there, that was the assignment. . . . We actually stayed a little longer, because the troops from the Baltic states refused to come. That's how it was. But I know people robbed the place, took out everything they could lift and carry. They transported the Zone back here. You can find it at the markets, the pawn shops, at people's dachas. The only thing that remained behind the wire was the land. And the graves. And our health. And our faith. Or my faith.

****

Our system, it's a military system, essentially, and it works great in emergencies. You're finally free there, and necessary. Freedom! And in those times the Russian shows how great he is. How unique. We'll never be Dutch or German. And we'll never have proper asphalt and manicured lawns. But there'll always be plenty of heroes.

Epilogue: Making Connections

The case studies in this book resemble the ancient Athenian tragedies. Athens' annual Dionysian festival presented trilogies (sets of three connected plays) that recast tragic myths and epic stories along lines that spoke to contemporary concerns, thereby providing a measure of catharsis for all who attended. In these four modern toxic waste tragedies, victims and their advocates gather every anniversary to restage and rewrite the tragedy of the accident. Public memory of these disasters remains contested and highly politicized, a contest that plays out today in the virtual world of the Internet. The tragedies contain multiple dramas: physical battles with the toxins, never-ending legal struggles, ritual burnings in effigy, and political skirmishes. Alongside and embedded within each of these dramas is the scientific drama. The scientific spectacle involves the search for evidence to show the health damage caused by the disaster, a search complicated by the reluctance of state authorities in all the case studies to track health and environmental data systematically and for long periods of time.

These ritual restagings of the tragedies help to forge a shared sense of suffering among the victims. In Bhopal, on every anniversary of the disaster, the community reaffirms its identity of victimization. They burn figures of Uncle Sam and of Union Carbide executives in effigy. Activists and sympathetic left-leaning journalists recount the story of victimization by an unjust, American-based multinational corporation. Greenpeace activists fly in from London, Brussels, and San Francisco to present visions of an alternative, more eco-friendly path to development. Local politicians join the chorus, conveniently ignoring the role of Indian officials and regulators in the disaster. In Niagara Falls, anniversaries of the tragedy bring back activists such as Lois Gibbs and Ralph Nader to the region to recount stories of suffering and injustice. Newspaper editors and columnists, the peddlers of the apocalypse, dutifully dredge up past news clippings and survivor stories. Chernobyl and Minamata have produced constituencies heavily invested in the commemoration of suffering and victimization. These dramas are captured in tales of woe and suffering, in documentaries, memoirs, monuments, oral histories, and memorial Web sites.

Nonetheless, despite all the drama, the passage of time ultimately favors a cooling of passions and a tendency toward historical amnesia. Most people, frankly, have forgotten about these disasters. And that is partly by design. Educational curricula, which almost everywhere are funded and designed by powerful state and economic interests, tend to omit stories that cast doubt on the possibility of negative outcomes from technological development. It is less a conspiracy than a refusal to confront evidence that modern history involves regress as well as progress, avoidable as well as necessary sacrifice. New York State does not include Love Canal on its high-school exit history exam for New York State history. Chernobyl is a distant and fading memory for young Russians, Belorussians, and Ukrainians. According to an expert on the presentation of Soviet history in Russian history textbooks, there is not a single mention of the Chernobyl accident, or of ecological and technological disasters in general, in state-approved social studies and history textbooks in the Russian Federation.[1] Bhopal barely gets mentioned, if at all, in any textbook of modern Indian history, though Bhopal activists have lobbied for years to include the disaster in the presentation of Indian

---

[1]E-mail correspondence with Vitaly Bezrogov, Senior Research Fellow, Russian Academy of Education, Moscow, March 27, 2009.

history in public schools. When it comes to episodes that encourage doubt and skepticism about technological progress, the tendency is toward historical amnesia, a condition that trumps even the most intense reminders of the disasters on the occasion of their anniversaries.

What it would take to incorporate technological and ecological disasters into state-approved curricula for high-school social studies and history courses? Is it naïve to expect state-funded systems of education to include information that might reflect unfavorably on the oft-repeated claim that technology and science make life more secure? Why is it that the most technologically adept societies in history are also beset by feelings of helplessness and insecurity?

AN EXCEPTION TO THE RULE

If there is one exception toward the more general trend toward historical amnesia, it is the case of Minamata. At least compared to the other societies in this book, Japanese political authorities were ultimately committed to remembering the disaster and teaching its lessons to future generations. Whereas the city of Niagara Falls categorically rejected any museum commemorating the Love Canal toxic waste disaster, Japan erected the Minamata Disease Municipal Museum in 1993 to teach the lessons of the tragedy. Unlike Union Carbide or Hooker Chemical Corporation, which never formally admitted guilt for the disasters at Bhopal and Niagara Falls, the Chisso Corporation publicly accepted its burden of guilt. In 2004, the Japanese government joined the chorus of apologizing and formally admitted responsibility for the spread of Minamata disease because of its failure to act in a timely fashion (conveniently, many argued, after decades of legal foot dragging and after most of the victims had died). Regardless, local and central governments in the United States and Bhopal, much less corporate entities, have never admitted any responsibility for the tragedies of Love Canal and Bhopal. All settlements stopped short of a formal declaration of guilt. There were victims but not perpetrators.

Alone among these case studies, Minamata seems to have prompted a fundamental shift in attitudes toward the environment and, indeed, in the very definition of progress. Japanese society went from a definition of progress that required and expected pollution as a necessary sacrifice to defining pollution as the antithesis of progress. New environmental laws accompanied this shift. In 1997, Japan became the focus for attempts to curb greenhouse gases, creating the framework of the Kyoto protocols. Japanese citizens were prepared, as polls suggested, to cut back on consumption in order to protect the environment. Why did Minamata contribute to such a turning point in attitudes and practices, while the other case studies did not? Was this shift a product of something unique to Japanese culture? What combination of grassroots activism, national cultural traditions, press coverage, and political leadership promoted new attitudes toward the environment? Readers might want to delve more deeply into each of this book's case studies to explain why the Japanese response in some fundamental ways differed from the response to other toxic-waste disasters. Of course, Japanese companies continue to foul the world's nest—just mostly on non-Japanese soil.

LANGUAGE AND METAPHOR

If Japan's uniqueness stands out, another striking problem, raised in all the case studies, has been the struggle to find the appropriate language and metaphors to describe each of the disasters. Beginning with Minamata and Love Canal, the disasters have shaped the images that people around the globe used to discuss toxic disaster. Russians and Ukrainians often called Chernobyl their Bhopal, just as Bhopal residents frequently dubbed Bhopal their Chernobyl or their Hiroshima. Even today, the disasters provide a convenient shorthand for unfathomable catastrophe. When Hurricane Katrina flooded dozens of toxic waste sites in the Mississippi Delta, broadcasters spoke of a new "Love Canal." In 2004, a U.S. Senator highlighted the vulnerability of the U.S. chemical industry to terrorist attack, noting that Al-Qaeda could do more "harm than Bhopal" by sabotaging a chemical plant. But have we gotten our metaphors right? Do these shorthands obscure as much as they reveal? How do historians explain massive suffering and damage that is the by-product of impersonal economic and technological forces and for which there is no clearly identifiable evil intent or motive? Calling such disasters a holocaust or genocide—a common tendency in all the societies of these case studies—ignores perhaps the most prominent attribute of all these catastrophes: unlike the Nazi gas chambers or the destruction of the Twin Towers on 9/11, no one intended that they happen. They were unintended consequences of progress.

TECHNOLOGICAL TRANSFERS AND THE WEB
OF CONNECTIONS

If all the case studies were unified by their accidental and unintended nature, they were also linked by a global process of environmental, technological, and political transformation. Consider the web of connections linking the disasters in this book. All four enterprises emerged from the science-intensive chemical industry of the nineteenth century. The industry was pioneered in Germany in the late nineteenth century and subsequently migrated to the United States, the Soviet Union, Japan, and the developing world. During the 1950s, the Chisso Corporation in Japan exploited the financial aid and credits offered by the United States following World War II and the dropping of atomic bombs on Hiroshima and Nagasaki. Soviet scientists used the same advances in the chemical industry that had spawned the U.S. chemical industry and nuclear power. While Soviet physicists developed much of the basic science to build a nuclear bomb on their own, they were aided by spies who collected information from within the U.S. Manhattan project to build the first atomic bombs. In addition, German chemists and physicists captured by the Soviets in their occupied territory of Germany after World War II helped develop the Soviet field of nuclear energy, just as German scientists in the American-occupied territory of Germany migrated to U.S. labs.

The web of connections also united the so-called "developed world" of the United States with newly independent nations in the "third world." Union Carbide, a U.S.-based corporation, had operations in Niagara Falls and maintained close ties with the company (Hooker Chemical Corporation) that caused the Love Canal disaster in the late 1970s. At the same time, Union Carbide had operated in India since the 1960s and was responsible for the massive toxic chemical leak that killed thousands in Bhopal, India, in December 1984. Bhopal was also a product of the green revolution of the 1960s to end hunger and famine in the third world. That effort, promoted by advisors from the United States and Soviet Union as part of their Cold War competition for the hearts, minds, and resources of the developing world, involved the construction of chemical plants in India to churn out pesticides and fertilizers, which undoubtedly contributed to the end of chronic famine in India but also set the stage for the Bhopal disaster in 1984. Each of these disasters thus came from a global nexus of modernization and technological development. That tangled nexus emerged from the intersection of profit-seeking conglomerates, the advancement of national programs of progress, and the large-scale transfers of technology and scientific expertise (through espionage, aid programs, and commercial transactions).

THE COST-BENEFIT CALCULUS OF PROGRESS

In all four case studies, political, business, and industry leaders claimed that environmental degradation was the price to pay for jobs, economic growth, and progress. Whether it was the Chernobyl plant in the Soviet Union or the chemical plant in Bhopal, civic and community leaders initially hailed their creations as stepping stone to a better future. Sure, there would have to be sacrifice, but that sacrifice was not to be in vain. The Indian prime minister Indira Gandhi famously announced to the first United Nations conference on the environment in 1972, "The worst pollution is poverty." It was precisely at this time that she allowed Union Carbide to expand its operations in Bhopal.

While societies got used to seeing pollution as unfortunate but inevitable and limited, those who questioned technological development were often denounced as "anti" progress. The mayor of Minamata in 1973 proclaimed to the disease-ridden community of fishermen he ostensibly was elected to represent: "What is good for Chisso [the company that dumped mercury into Minamata Bay] is good for Minamata." It was a variation on the famous claim of the head of General Motors in the United States in 1953 that "what is good for the country is good for General Motors and vice versa." A Bhopal activist in 2008 told this author that the Union Carbide plant was built in his city in the 1970s with no public input about potential safety impacts because, "No one could be opposed to development."[2] Those who questioned development were immediately dubbed "antiprogress" and called "Luddites" (a pejorative term for a group of individuals in early nineteenth-century Great Britain who smashed and vandalized the textile machines that had displaced them from their jobs). Only those who supported economic growth

---

[2]Interview with Abdul Jabbar, a Bhopal victims' activist, July 8, 2008.

FIGURE E.1   Demonstrators in front of the Bhopal factory compound in July 2008. (Andrew L. Jenks)

and development had a political voice, a feature shared by all the societies in this study.

The inability to argue against progress, at least in part, contributed to all four of the disasters. In Bhopal, state and local officials, working with the multinational corporation Union Carbide, easily overrode weakly articulated local objections to the creation of the Bhopal chemical plant in 1969. The fishermen of Minamata were expected to sacrifice their livelihood and heritage for the sake of the more "progressive" and "modern" industry that settled in the area and began dumping mercury into the waters. When Love Canal residents in the mid-1970s began complaining to journalists about noxious substances percolating into their backyard and destroying their health, local politicians condemned them for giving the reputation of the city, and thus its potential for attracting tourists, new residents, and new industry, a bad name.

The dominant doctrine of progress created a cost-benefit ledger in which a clean environment and operational safety were calculated

FIGURE E.2   Graffiti on the walls surrounding the Bhopal factory compound in July 2008. "Dow Chemical Must End Toxic Terror in Bhopal." (Andrew L. Jenks)

as costs of development and not a benefit. Since everyone seemed to agree that costs were things to be reduced, outlays on safety and waste management were therefore cut to the barest possible minimum. Treating safety as a cost rather than a benefit contributed to each of the disasters in this book; it also constituted a shared belief that connected seemingly disparate societies and cultures in twentieth-century world history. Would it be possible to design a global formula for progress that would consider industrial safety a benefit rather than a cost, and therefore something to be maximized rather than minimized?

DISASTERS AS CULTURAL MIRRORS

While this book provides a window into common transnational attitudes about the trade-offs and costs of progress, the disasters also reveal key differences between the societies. In the case of Chernobyl, for instance, the disaster encouraged very little immediate civic activism or demands for a fundamental restructuring of power relationships. The reason was that nearly seven decades of Soviet rule had effectively destroyed nonstate traditions of organization, charity, and political association in Soviet society. All media outlets were controlled by the state and forced to print, broadcast, and air only the official government position. As a result, Soviet victims of Chernobyl had to depend entirely upon the inadequate response of their government, whose officials, for nearly two weeks, denied that the disaster had even happened.

The United States, unlike the Soviet Union, had nonstate structures that filled at least some of the vacuum of governmental incompetence and waffling: churches, charitable organizations, grass-roots activists, and newspaper reporters willing to report something other than the official government and corporate positions. Those structures operated as a kind of immune-response system, as they did also in the case of the Minamata mercury poisoning in Japan. Tapping a tradition of grass-roots activism, citizens in Japan and the United States, and to a lesser extent in India, forced the government to confront some of its failures (though by no means all of them). They also hired lawyers to force corporate polluters to provide at least some compensation. The Soviet Union, in stark contrast, had no legal system through which citizens could sue polluters, especially since the state was the polluter and controlled all courts and judges.

Differences also emerged in the way each of the societies made sense of the disasters. When people discussed Love Canal, Chernobyl, Bhopal, or Minamata, they drew from their own society's way of understanding the world: its villains and heroes, its prescriptions for dealing with risk and danger, and its perception of power and gender. For instance, Soviet eyewitnesses of the Chernobyl explosion imagined themselves as soldiers fighting the Nazi scourge in the Great Patriotic War, the title by which Russians know World War II. Battling nature, in their mind, was just like making war with Fascism. As a result, many laid down their lives to vanquish the scourge of Chernobyl, just as their parents and grandparents had died to defend the Soviet Union from the Nazis. When Japanese fishermen in the 1950s began suffering the debilitating effects of mercury poisoning, like the Soviets they drew from their own culture to understand the situation. Many imagined that the condition was punishment by the *kami*, or spirits, for a violation of the proper balance between humans and the natural world—destroyed by a relentless process of industrial and economic development in Japan since the nineteenth century. Other Japanese fishermen saw the strange disease as a test of their manhood, which they should suffer in samurai-like, stoic silence, steeling themselves with strong shots of the sweet potato vodka *shochu*. Their shame at losing their sense of manhood made them reluctant to reveal their condition and to ask for help. In Bhopal, the vast majority of victims—residents of slums surrounding the Union Carbide plant—were Muslims, who had experienced discrimination and exploitation at the hands of the majority Hindu population of India. The effect of the disaster was thus to intensify dramatically existing religious and class tensions in the city, creating a divide in the minds of many between poor "Muslim" victims and wealthy non-Muslim perpetrators (American and Hindu). Meanwhile, the residents of Niagara Falls understood the Love Canal disaster as a direct challenge to the American dream of home ownership and to the family home as a physical and financial line of defense against a dangerous world. They understood justice as a government buyout of their house and a subsidized loan to purchase another home. Unlike many Indians in Bhopal or Soviet citizens in Chernobyl, who had a far lower standard of living, Niagara Falls residents had the American sense of confidence that lost material goods could and should be replaced or even bettered. A comparative examination of four distinct industrial disasters can therefore illuminate the conditions that distinguish societies and political systems across the globe—as well as the factors that unite them.

DISASTER IMAGINATIONS

Regardless of social and cultural context, people considered large-scale disaster and death-dealing smog exceptional and uncharacteristic. The belief that large-scale disaster was exceptional rather than normal meant that governments and communities did not prepare for them—in India, the Soviet Union, Japan, or the United States. "How can you believe in something incomprehensible?" asked one Chernobyl victim, in response to an interviewer's question about Chernobyl. The explosion of the reactor at Chernobyl was so unexpected that when firemen arrived to put out chunks of burning graphite and uranium, they discovered that city planners had not installed a fire hydrant near the plant. When the Love Canal crisis became a national news story and full-blown political emergency, an aide to President Jimmy Carter remarked, "Love Canal did not fit any category for which there was a policy." When the Bhopal plant ushered forth a toxic cloud of chemicals, Union Carbide officials, much less the local police, had no idea what impact the chemicals might have on human health or if there was even an antidote. The chief of police in Bhopal at the time of the disaster, one of the first responders, told this author in the summer of 2008. "When you look back you wish that Union Carbide, and all of us, had more concern for the people living around the plant, some kind of information system where you could have alerted people . . . some system . . . of mock exercises, mock drills, [information about] where to go, when to go, the hospital to go to, the antidotes, how to manage, who to contact. There was none of that."[3] The inability to imagine each of the disasters greatly exacerbated the tragic consequences of the disasters. Used to thinking of progress in terms of best-case scenarios for the future, people in charge did not ask hard questions about safety and the environment *until after* the unthinkable had occurred and it was too late.

Each of the societies consistently overestimated the benefits of progress and underestimated the costs. They all subscribed to an overarching metaideology of progress that exuded an optimism bordering on hubris and overconfidence. They all believed that catastrophic technological failure, leading to social and political crisis, was something that happened somewhere else. In short, they all lacked the ability to imagine the unthinkable and to prepare for it, another common attitude that connected all the seemingly different societies and political systems discussed in this book.

Finally, each of the disasters raised the problem of finding appropriate ways to compensate victims for their suffering. Invariably, the identification of suffering was an economic and political process that required asking and answering a gruesome question: How much is a human life worth? Can the magnitude of a disaster be measured in the number of deaths? Is suffering, from a legal point of view, purely physical? Is psychological damage "real" and if so, can it be quantified? Among other things, putting the problem of suffering into economic terms allowed many to claim that victims were attempting

---

[3]Interview with Swaraj Puri, the former chief of police in Bhopal, July 9, 2008.

to exploit the system for their own gain. Those who did not receive money resented those who did—and many concluded that displays of suffering were staged and inauthentic. It didn't help that there were many fake victims in Bhopal and elsewhere, unscrupulous con artists adept at working their respective systems. Stories of the exploits of pretend victims—or suspicions that some victims looked too healthy to really be victims—cheapened the suffering of many "real" victims, who often received no compensation, moral or material. Systems of compensation also created a vested interest in maximizing the scope of the disaster, just as those who caused the disasters had a vested interest in minimizing their impact. While acknowledging the contradictory motives of perpetrators and polluters—and resisting the temptation to represent them as irredeemably evil—is it also possible to acknowledge and analyze the complex motivations of victims—and resisting the temptation to represent them as saints and martyrs?

As the scholar Ulrich Beck has noted, people live in the new age of the "risk society." In this new era, the distribution of risk has become as politically explosive as the distribution of wealth. The challenge is to develop ways to involve society in the operation, maintenance, and regulation of risky enterprises, an especially difficult proposition given the highly technical nature of modern industry. While citizens must become more technically literate, engineers and scientists must understand and accept the political and ethical implications of their knowledge and learn to communicate their knowledge in plain language. They must also learn to recognize the limits of their capabilities—and to entertain the possibility that some large-scale technological enterprises, as the sociologist Charles Perrow has suggested, are simply too complex and too dangerous to deploy. To what extent have societies developed mechanisms of control and oversight since the disasters discussed in this book? And to what extent have scientific and technical communities developed a language capable of bridging the gap between themselves and the rest of society?

Bibliography

GENERAL WORKS ON TECHNOLOGY AND ENVIRONMENT

Two seminal essays have shaped the scholarly conception of the relationship between technological modernization and the environment: Garrett Hardin, "The Tragedy of the Commons," *Science* 162 (1968): 1243–1248; and Lynn White, "The Historical Roots of Our Ecological Crisis," *Science* 155 (1967): 1203–1207. Hardin argues that individuals acting in their own economic self-interest, a distinctive feature of capitalist modernity, develop a destructive and exploitative attitude toward shared natural resources. White believes that destructive practices toward the environment are rooted in culture and not just in economics. He suggests that Christianity created a view of nature as a resource to be exploited rather than as an object to be worshipped and deified. Another study that explores the aesthetic, cultural, and religious motivations for large-scale technological transformation is Thomas P. Hughes, *Human-Built World: How to Think about Technology and Culture* (Chicago, IL: University of Chicago Press, 2004). Hughes refers to European transformations of nature as a "second creation," an attempt to imitate God. One limitation in all these works is that they tend to be Eurocentric or focused on the U.S. experience. Another historian has attempted to tease out the relationship between political systems and the environment in a broader world context, arguing that authoritarian regimes tend to be more destructive of environmental resources than political systems with a strong civil society: Paul Josephson, *Resources under Regimes: Technology, Environment, and the State* (Cambridge, MA: Harvard University Press, 2004). See also Paul Josephson, *Industrialized Nature* (Washington, D.C.: Island Press, 2002). Another work with a broader world focus examines the relationship between ideologies of progress, modernizing states, and large-scale technological and social engineering projects that have gone horribly wrong: James Scott, *Seeing Like a State: How Certain Schemes to Improve the Human Condition Have Failed* (New Haven, CT: Yale University Press, 1998). Another influential attempt to explain the general principles behind massive technological failure suggests that technological disasters are "normal" attributes of modern technological systems: Charles Perrow, *Normal Accidents: Living with High-Risk Technologies* (New York: Basic Books, 1984). See also Edward Tenner, *Why Things Bite Back: Technology and the Revenge of Unintended Consequences* (New York: Vintage Books, 1997). For a general overview of the environment and world history, see J. R. McNeill, *Something New Under the Sun: An Environmental History of the Twentieth Century World* (New York: W.W. Norton & Co., 2001). For various approaches to ecological and technological disaster, see Angus Gunn, *Unnatural Disasters: Case Studies of Human-Induced Environmental Catastrophes* (Westport, CT: Greenwood Press, 2003); and Anthony Oliver Smith and Susanna M. Hoffman, eds., *The Angry Earth: Disaster in Anthropological Perspective* (New York: Routledge, 1999). On the various ways communities react to ecological disaster, see James K. Mitchell, *The Long Road to Recovery: Community Responses to Industrial Disaster* (New York and Tokyo: United Nations Press, 1996). For discussions of the relationship between conceptions of risk and blame in a modern technological society, Ulrich Beck, *Risk Society: Towards a New Modernity*, trans. M. Ritter (London: Sage Publications, 1992); and Mary Douglas, *Risk and Blame: Essays in Cultural Theory* (London: Routledge, 1992). Both authors have been influential in drawing attention to the social and political construction of risk. Another prominent sociologist explores the paradox that the most technologically adept societies are the ones that feel most insecure about their environment: Zygmunt

Bauman, *Liquid Fear* (Malden, MA: Polity Press, 2006). On the origins of the modern conception of pollution and its relationship to the industrial revolution, politics, science, and culture, see Peter Thorsheim, *Inventing Pollution: Coal, Smoke, and Culture in Britain since 1800* (Athens, OH: Ohio University Press, 2006). The book tracks the shift in nineteenth-century Great Britain from the view that pollution is caused by nature to the idea that pollution is man made—a shift that parallels current debates over whether global warming is a natural or man-made phenomenon. To examine the relationship between technological mastery, domination of the natural world, and European Imperialism, see Michael Adas, *Machines as the Measure of Men: Science, Technology, and Ideologies of Western Dominance* (Ithaca, NY: Cornell University Press, 1989); and Gabrielle Hecht and Paul Edwards, *The Technopolitics of Cold War: Toward a Transregional Perspective* (Washington, D.C.: American Historical Association, 2007). The latter work also illustrates the importance of large-scale technological projects in the construction of modern identities in the twentieth century. The politicization of expertise and science is explored in Theodore Porter, *Trust in Numbers: The Pursuit of Objectivity in Science and Public Life* (Princeton, NJ: Princeton University Press, 1996). The idea of the "unspoken bargain," whereby workers accepted a degraded environment in exchange for jobs, is discussed in Hal Rothman, *Saving the Planet: The American Response to the Environment in the Twentieth Century* (Chicago, IL: Ivan R. Dee, 2000). A useful overview of environmental degradation in modern world history is presented in Miguel A. Santos, *The Environmental Crisis* (Westport, CT: Greenwood Press, 1999).

MINAMATA

A general discussion of pollution in modern Japan, which also includes a discussion of Minamata, is presented in Jun Ui, ed., *Industrial Pollution in Japan* (Tokyo: United Nations University Press, 1992). Another overview of pollution in modern Japan is Ken'ichi Miyamoto, *The Characteristic Features of Japanese Pollution Problems* (Osaka: Osaka City University, 1979). Margaret A. McKean, *Environmental Protest and Citizen Politics in Japan* (Berkeley, CA: University of California Press, 1981), examines the relationship between the environmental movement and a more general democratization of

Japanese politics after World War II. The definitive scholarly account of the Minamata disaster in English is Timothy S. George, *Minamata: Pollution and the Struggle for Democracy in Postwar Japan* (Cambridge, MA: Harvard University Asia Center, 2001). George illustrates the importance of Minamata in a more general mobilization of grassroots democracy in Japan. A Japanese journalist's account of the disaster is Akio Mishima, *Bitter Sea: The Human Cost of Minamata Disease*, trans. Richard Gage and Susan Murata (Tokyo: Kosei Publishing Co., 1992). One of the most important publications in drawing worldwide attention to Minamata disease was an essay and collection of photographs on the plight of Minamata disease sufferers: W. Eugene Smith and Aileen M. Smith, *Minamata* (New York: Holt, Rinehart and Winston, 1975). The pictures in this book were featured in exhibits shown around the world in the 1970s. The most important publication on Minamata within Japan, written by a shy housewife from Minamata whose transformation into an activist parallels in some ways the biography of Lois Gibbs at Love Canal, is Ishimure Michiko, *Paradise in the Sea of Sorrow: Our Minamata Disease*, trans. Livia Monnet (Ann Arbor, MI: University of Michigan Center for Japanese Studies, 2003). An anthropological perspective on pollution and Minamata disease is contained in Kazuko Tsurumi, *Social Price of Pollution in Japan and the Role of Folk Beliefs* (Tokyo: Sophia University, 1977); and Kazuko Tsurumi, *New Lives: Some Case Studies in Minamata* (Tokyo: Sophia University, 1988). For a very moving and insightful memoir from a Minamata disease sufferer, see Oiwa Keibo, narrated by Ogata Masato, *Rowing the Eternal Sea: The Story of a Minamata Fisherman*, trans. Karen Colligan-Taylor (New York: Rowman & Littlefield, 2001). A somewhat technical exploration of the condition of Minamata disease is presented in Masazumi Harada, *Minamata Disease* (Kumamoto, Japan: Kumamoto Nichinichi Shinbun Culture & Information Center, 2004); and Tadao Takeuchi and Komyo Eto, *The Pathology of Minamata Disease: A Tragic Story of Water Pollution* (Fukuoka: Kyushu University Press, 1999). The Ministry of Environment, government of Japan, presents the official government history of Minamata in English: http://www.env.go.jp/en/chemi/hs/minamata2002/. The Chisso Corporation, which today produces high definition displays for televisions and computers, does not mention Minamata disease in its English-language Web site's discussion of the company's history: http://www.chisso.co.jp/english/company/time_line.html.

LOVE CANAL

For the most recent scholarly history of Love Canal, see Elizabeth D. Blum, *Love Canal Revisited: Race, Class, and Gender in Environmental Activism* (Lawrence, KA: University Press of Kansas, 2008). As the title suggests, the book focuses on the social and political impacts of the disaster. The person for whom Love Canal was named presented his scheme (a plan for a "Model City") to create a new community in and around Niagara Falls in William T. Love, *Description and Plan of the Model City Located at Lewiston, Niagara County, N.Y. Chartered by Special Act of the New York Legislature. Designed to be the Most Perfect City in Existence* (Lewiston, NY: The Model Town Company, 1893). It is ironic, of course, that a "Model City" plan would turn into a toxic dump. For the history of Model City, see also Rich Newman, "From Love's Canal to Love Canal: Reckoning with the Environmental Legacy of an Industrial Dream," in *Beyond the Ruins: The Meanings of Deindustrialization*, ed., Jefferson Cowie and Joseph Heathcott (Ithaca, NY: Cornell University Press, 2003), 112–135. On the relationship between Love Canal and the construction of urban utopias, as well as the link between Love Canal and the Manhattan Project, see Andrew Jenks, "Model City USA: The Environmental Cost of Victory in World War II and the Cold War," *Environmental History* 12 (2007): 552–577. New York State investigated the issue of radioactive wastes in Love Canal in the following report: *The Federal Connection: A History of U.S. Military Involvement in the Toxic Contamination of Love Canal and the Niagara Frontier Region*. An Interim Report to New York State Assembly Speaker Stanley Fink, 2 vols (Albany, NY: New York State Assembly Task Force on Toxic Substances, January 29, 1981). On environmental activism and gender issues in Niagara Falls as a result of Love Canal, see Rich Newman, "Making Environmental Politics: Women and Love Canal Activism," *Women's Studies Quarterly* 29 (2001): 65–84. Adeline Gordon Levine, *Love Canal: Science, Politics, and People* (Lexington, MA: D.C. Heath and Company, 1982), discusses the struggle of Love Canal activists as well as the political manipulation of scientific data and expertise by state and federal authorities. The most interesting and informative memoir from an eyewitness is Lois Gibbs, *Love Canal: The Story Continues* (Stony Creek, CT: New Society Publishers, 1998). Gibbs recounts the grassroots environmental activism of lower-middle-class residents as well as her own transformation from a shy and retiring housewife into a national political activist. Thomas Fletcher, *From Love Canal to Environmental Justice: The*

Politics of Hazardous Waste on the Canada-U.S. Border (Peterborough, Ontario: Broadview Press, 2003), explores the transnational implications of Love Canal, since the city of Niagara Falls is on the border with Canada. Systems of toxic waste management that contributed to the Love Canal disaster are explored in Craig E. Colten and Peter N. Skinner, *The Road to Love Canal: Managing Industrial Waste before EPA* (Austin, TX: University of Texas Press, 1996). Allan Mazur, *The Rashomon Effect: A Hazardous Inquiry* (Cambridge, MA: Harvard University Press, 1998), presents the contradictory views on Love Canal from the perspective of various corporate, government, and activist eyewitnesses. Eric Zuesse, "Love Canal: The Truth Seeps Out," *Reason* 12 (1981): 16–33, argues that local government officials, rather than the Hooker Chemical Corporation, bore the primary responsibility for the Love Canal disaster by permitting residential development in an area they knew to be contaminated. Students interested in examining primary source documents related to Love Canal should consult the Love Canal Collection, State University of New York, Buffalo: http://ublib.buffalo.edu/libraries/specialcollections/lovecanal/.

BHOPAL

For a general account of development in India and its impact on the environment, see Madhav Gadgil and Ramachandra Guha, *This Fissured Land: An Ecological History of India* (Berkeley, CA: University of California Press, 1993); and Madhav Gadgil and Ramachandra Guha, *The Use and Abuse of Nature* (New Delhi: Oxford University Press, 2000). Changing conceptions of risk after Bhopal are explored in Sheila Jasanoff, ed., *Learning from Disaster: Risk Management after Bhopal* (Philadelphia, PA: University of Pennsylvania Press, 1994). Transnational technology transfers and the political and legal challenges they presented are discussed in Sheila Jasanoff, "Bhopal's Trials of Knowledge and Ignorance," *Isis* 98 (2007): 344–450. The legal battles that ensued after the disaster are discussed in Jamie Cassels, *The Uncertain Promise of Law: Lessons from Bhopal* (Toronto: University of Toronto Press, 1993). Paul Shrivastava, *Bhopal: Anatomy of a Crisis* (Cambridge, MA: Ballinger Publishing, 1987), examines the disaster from the perspective of corporate and governmental crisis management. An excellent journalistic account of the crisis is contained in Dominic Lapierre and Javier Moro, *Five Past Midnight in Bhopal: The Epic Story of the World's Worst Industrial Disaster* (New York: Warner Books, 2002). Another account from the *New York*

Times correspondent who covered the accident at the time is Sanjoy Hazarika, *Bhopal: The Lessons of a Tragedy* (New York: Viking Penguin, 1987). The impact of Bhopal on environmental activism is explored in Kim Fortun, *Advocacy after Bhopal: Environmentalism, Disaster, New Global Orders* (Chicago, IL: University of Chicago Press, 2001). Whether or not the Bhopal disaster was an accident or a deliberate act is discussed in Brojendra Banerjee, *Bhopal Gas Tragedy: Accident or Experiment* (New Delhi: Paribus Publishers, 1986). An account that attempts to identify the factors that led to Bhopal, and which have also contributed to other disasters, is David Weir, *The Bhopal Syndrome* (San Francisco, CA: Sierra Club Books, 1987). Interviews with workers at the Union Carbide plant are contained in T. Chouhan et al., eds., *Bhopal: The Inside Story, Carbide Workers Speak Out on the World's Worst Industrial Disaster* (New York: Apex Press, 1994). An excellent collection of primary source documents is Bridget Hanna et al., eds., *The Bhopal Reader: Remembering Twenty Years of the World's Worst Industrial Disaster* (New York: Apex Press, 2005). For an analysis of the U.S. media's treatment of the Bhopal disaster, see Lee Wilkens, *Shared Vulnerability: The Media and American Perceptions of the Bhopal Disaster* (New York: Greenwood Press, 1987). For information about Bhopal victims today and for general information about the disaster, see the Web site of the main nongovernmental clinic located in the midst of the slums of Bhopal: http://www.bhopal.org/sambhavnaclinic.html. For the official Union Carbide position on all aspects of the disaster: http://www.bhopal.com/.

CHERNOBYL

A moving and engrossing oral history of the disaster, which contains testimony from various victims of the disaster and their relatives, is presented in Svetlana Alexievich, *Voices from Chernobyl: The Oral History of a Nuclear Disaster*, trans. Keith Gessen (New York: Picador Macmillan, 2006). For a positive, officially sanctioned spin on the Chernobyl disaster from the Soviet authorities, see Vasil Nibak, *Chernobyl: Truth and Inventions* (Kiev: Politvidav Ukraini Publishers, 1987). One prominent Ukrainian author and medical doctor interviewed numerous eyewitnesses and produced the following account: Iurii Shcherbak, *Chernobyl: A Documentary Story*, trans. Ian Press (New York: St. Martin's Press, 1989). A collection of interviews with Ukrainian politicians and nationalists on the subject of Chernobyl is provided by Roman Solchanyk, ed., *Ukraine: From Chernobyl' to Sovereignty* (New York: St. Martin's Press, 1992). Official attempts to cover up the accident are explored by an investigative journalist in Alla Yaroshinskaya, *Chernobyl: The Forbidden Truth*, trans. Michele Kan and Julia Sallabank (Lincoln NB: University of Nebraska Press, 1995). A Soviet nuclear power expert who worked at the plant wrote a minute-by-minute account of the events leading to the disaster: Grigori Medvedev, *The Truth about Chernobyl* (New York: Basic Books, 1991). An excellent summary of the accident and collection of documents and photographs is contained in Richard Mould, *Chernobyl, The Real Story* (New York: Pergamon Press, 1988). Some of the best scholarly accounts of various aspects of the Chernobyl disaster are David Marples, *Chernobyl and Nuclear Power in the USSR* (New York: St. Martin's Press, 1986); and David Marples, *The Social Impact of the Chernobyl Disaster* (New York: St. Martin's Press, 1988). An anthropologist has examined the politics of suffering, risk, medicine, and science in the aftermath of Chernobyl: Adriana Petryna, *Life Exposed: Biological Citizens after Chernobyl* (Princeton, NJ: Princeton University Press, 2002). Mary Mycio, *Wormwood Forest: A Natural History of Chernobyl* (Washington, D.C.: Joseph Henry Press, 2005), investigates the paradox that the abandoned zone around the Chernobyl plant has become one of the largest de facto wildlife sanctuaries in Europe. On the broader importance of technological mastery in legitimizing Soviet political authority (which Chernobyl directly threatened), see Andrew Jenks, "A Metro on the Mount: The Underground as a Church of Soviet Civilization," *Technology and Culture* 44 (2000): 697–724. The article also examines the origins of the reckless, risk-taking style of technological management that contributed to the disaster. Loren Graham, *The Ghost of the Executed Engineer: Technology and the Fall of the Soviet Union* (Cambridge, MA: Harvard University Press, 1993), examines the relationship between the collapse of the Soviet Union and technological failure and includes a discussion of the Chernobyl disaster. Robert Polidori and Elizabeth Culbert, *Zones of Exclusion: Pripyat and Chernobyl* (Gottingen: Steidl, 2003) is a fascinating collection of images of the contaminated zone in the years after the accident. The relationship between Chernobyl and the rise of anti-Soviet nationalism in Ukraine and elsewhere is discussed in Jane Dawson, *Eco-Nationalism: Anti-Nuclear Activism and National Identity in Russia, Lithuania and Ukraine* (Durham, NC: Duke University Press, 1996). For a somewhat technical examination of the environmental impacts of the Chernobyl accident and other ecological catastrophes of the Soviet era, see Murray Feshbach, *Ecological Disaster: Cleaning up the Hidden Legacy of the Soviet Regime* (New York: Twentieth Century Fund Press, 1995).

Index